Shift Happens!

21 Days to Better Energy
Through the Chakras

An Interactive Guidebook by
Arielle Sterling

Shift Happens!

21 Days to Better Energy through the Chakras

An Interactive Guidebook

By Arielle Sterling

First Edition July 2016

ISBN: **1530630355**
ISBN-13: 978-1530630356

Disclaimer: This book is not intended as a substitute for the medical advice of physicians. The reader should regularly consult a physician in matters relating to his/her health and particularly with respect to any symptoms that may require diagnosis or medical attention. Before beginning any new diet or exercise program it is recommended that you seek medical advice from your personal physician. If you have any medical conditions, check with your doctor before performing any kind of detox. Hot baths are not recommended for people with high blood pressure.

Spiritual Beliefs: There are a myriad of cultures and spiritual orientations that use different words to express an understanding of the miracle of consciousness or existence. In this book, this understanding is expressed with different words and phrases such as, "Source", "Divine" or "Spirit". I encourage you to use the terminology that suits your beliefs best.

DEDICATION

This book is dedicated to anyone who has ever felt uncomfortable in their own skin. Your essence is your soul; your body, simply the vessel. Being human doesn't have to be hard if you don't want it to be.

TABLE OF CONTENTS

PREFACE

Welcome to *Shift Happens! 21 Days to Better Energy Through the Chakras*, an interactive guidebook! I created this book to share with you my story, my knowledge of the chakras and show you the tools that you can use to take charge of your body and your energy, chakra by chakra. This experience has been designed as a 21 day journey to allow yourself the time to process this information, build upon your knowledge and self-care skills, and find ways that work for you to implement them into your daily life. The goal is to learn how to be proactive with maintaining your energy instead of having to be reactive. When I was younger, I wasn't equipped to deal with the energy that was surrounding me, good or bad. I had to learn to support myself through maintaining healthy energy and chakras. I hope to share with you my tools so that you too can balance your mind, body and spirit and take your life to new heights that you can control.

I am a highly sensitive person. Growing up, I was constantly told I was *too sensitive* and that I would need to grow a thicker skin if I wanted to "make it in the world". Signs of my lack of energetic control were everywhere and affected almost every single aspect of my life. I had no control over my energy or my life. I was constantly sick, tired and depressed. And bless my parents' hearts, but they had no idea what the hell to do with me. Their parents antiquated methods of parenting could never have prepared them for me. I was *different*.

As a teenager, I came into the awareness that I was an empath, and it became apparent that I didn't need to grow a thicker skin, I needed to gain control of my energy and energetic boundaries. I had zero boundaries, so I soaked everything up like a sponge, making me feel all of the pain and suffering in the world around me. I had become so clouded by everything around me that I became depressed and was completely disillusioned. I couldn't see a future for myself, I couldn't interact properly with people, I couldn't feel anything but anger, hurt and fear. And then, I couldn't feel anything. I was in a state of eternal numbness. Wondering if I would ever feel again, I began to cut myself. By the time I reached out for help, my parents had no choice but to admit me to an in-patient treatment program.

After spending about two weeks in intensive therapy, it became apparent how crucial it was for me to take charge of my own health and happiness. The medications I was given completely dulled my personality, squashed my energy and severely limited my brain function. I was a shell of myself. I knew that I needed figure out what was going on with me instead being dependent on something outside of me for the rest of my life. I didn't want to turn into the people I saw around me that needed a substance (alcohol, drugs, prescription medication, etc.) to just get through their lives.

I started learning about Reiki and other forms of energy healing, which all seemed to be centered in this idea that the energy around you affects your mind, body and spirit, along with this energetic system called the chakras. Educating myself about the chakras was the gateway to understanding my own energy and how it affected not only my body, but my entire existence. I understood how important it was to control the energy that I let into my space, the energy that I chose to surround myself with; what I truly let impact my being. That was when I started to take my life back, along with my personal power.

Fast forward to my mid-twenties, when I started teaching about metaphysics, I found the most popular class was about the chakra system. People wanted to know how to implement spiritual tools into their lives to honor their chakras. This guidebook was inspired by those chakra classes, along with some other gems I've picked up along the way. These are the things that have helped me in learning to maintain my own energy and have allowed me to transform my life! I am more clear, my natural discernment is stronger, and I am able to actually feel my own energy. I am in tune with my body, able to listen to the whispers it provides instead of waiting to hear the screams. I have a stronger sense of myself and my connection to the Universe. I no longer hesitate to speak my truth, yet I am in better control of what I used to consider a sharp-tongue. My senses are heightened and I find signals of my alignment with the Universe daily.

Every individual is unique, and each experience is distinct, but by taking these next three weeks to learn about your chakras, you are making a lasting commitment to you and your health. Thank you for joining me on this journey. I am truly honored to be apart of your personal awakening. Are you ready? Because remember, *shift happens*!

    With Infinite Love and Light,
        xo Arielle Sterling

INTRODUCTION

This guidebook has a number of unique features to help support you on your 21 day journey and beyond. Each of the seven main chakras is broken down into a 3 day chapter. Each chapter begins with a brief quiz to help you determine if that chakra may be imbalanced. If you answer yes to any of the questions, that is an indication that the chakra may not be operating at its full potential and provide a clue as to the deeper cause of any imbalance(s).

At the beginning of each of the seven chakra chapters, you will see the following information:

1

2   3
MULADHARA | I AM

4	Color	Red
5	Element	Earth
6	Ruled By	Saturn
7	Gemstones	Hematite, Black Tourmaline, Red Jasper, Garnet, Ruby, Bloodstone, Onyx, Tiger's Eye, Obsidian
8	Essential Oils	Ylang ylang, Cedar Atlas, Juniper, Vetiver, Cinnamon, Patchouli, Spikenard, Nutmeg, Ginger, Myrrh
9	Note/Frequency	C / 7.8 Hz
10	Mantra	Lam

1. **Image** – Each chakra has a different number of petals and contains unique symbolism. The image shown is a common representation of the chakra, but there are many different variations ranging from basic to deeply intricate.
2. **Name** – The name of the chakra is listed in Sanskrit, the language of origin. Chakra are also commonly referred to by their location on the body.
3. **Affirmation** – This is the positive statement that resonates to the energy of the chakra.
4. **Color** – Each chakra resonates to a specific color of the visible light spectrum (red, orange, yellow, green, blue, indigo, violet). However, there are some chakra that may resonate with more than one color.
5. **Element** – Every chakra resonates with an element (Earth, Air, Water, etc.). This element may provide clues as to the best way to connect with that chakra.
6. **Ruled By** – The Chakra system can be correlated with the planetary system. If there is an astrological upset with a planet, chances are you may be experiencing either a physiological or emotionally related flare up in one of your chakra if they are unbalanced.
7. **Gemstones** – Every gemstone carries metaphysical healing properties along with the ability to help align the chakra system. The color of the stone typically correlates with the chakra it helps to bring back into perfection.
8. **Essential Oils** – Every living being resonates at a certain vibration, plants included. The essence and vibration of the plant is captured in its essential oil for convenience and ease of usage. The essential oils listed resonate around the frequency of the chakra and work to bring it into alignment.
9. **Note / Frequency** – When the chakra is operating in perfection it will be open and operating at a specific frequency. By playing this note or any tune in that key, you can immediately begin to restore balance.
10. **Mantra** – This is the sacred sound that is associated with each chakra. This is often used repetitively in mediation to focus energy to the specific chakra.

Within each chapter you will learn about what each chakra's function is within the physical body as well as its relationship with your emotions. You will discover what it can affect in your physical body, and what symptoms may arise as an under or over active chakra. Most importantly, you will learn about all of the tools that you can use to help balance out your own chakra. Each day of your 21 day journey has a meditative activity for you to connect to the chakra in a new and unique way. After the day's exercise, you will take some time to reflect on that day's experience.

In addition to each of the 21 days of meditation, there are a number of additional meditative ideas and exercises included in the book that can be used to enhance your experience. There are a number of interactive tools related to your toolbox, providing fresh ideas for applying them in your daily life. At the end of the book, you will find some extra journal and coloring pages for additional thoughts, ideas and artistic expressions of color that may come to you during your journey.

In this guidebook, I will be discussing the connection that we have to a higher power. I will typically use the terms Source and the Universe, but know that for those of you who have a relationship with the Divine, when I mention Source, this will be indicative of your connection with God.

TOOLBOX

You are perfect, whole and complete just as you are. This guidebook is a tool for you to use to bring awareness to your body and your energy in a new way. There are a number of other tools at your disposal to help aid in clearing and balancing your chakra. Once you have gained the awareness as to how each chakra affects your body, it will be easier for you to make lifestyle adjustments in order to have better energy and maintain balanced chakras on a regular basis. Here are some ideas of how you can address your energy!

ॐ **Food** is energy! You eat to nourish your physical body energy, so why not feed your energetic body as well? Eating specific foods that are coordinated with specific chakra can assist in boosting chakra function!

ॐ **Water** is liquid energy! By staying hydrated, energy is able to move easily throughout the body. If the body is not properly hydrated, the body's natural flow of energy is disrupted and it cannot function to its highest potential. This is one of the most important (and easiest to forget about) steps in maintaining healthy energy.

ॐ **Baths** can be used as a physical method to cleanse the energy of all of your chakra simultaneously. Since water is liquid energy, immersing yourself in it is the perfect use! Salt baths can be used to help draw out impurities and toxins in the body and help blocked energy to move.

ॐ Each chakra resonates with a certain **color** of the rainbow. By surrounding yourself with the color that is aligned to the chakra, you can easily get an extra boost! You can try wearing the color on clothes, jewelry or even colored lenses on sun glasses!

ॐ **Gemstones** are living energies that grow from elements of the Earth, each carrying a specific metaphysical purpose and frequency. They are often used by placing them on their corresponding chakras, meditating while holding the stone or worn on jewelry.

ॐ Plants are medicinal in nature and hold healing properties associated with the frequencies they carry. **Aromatherapy** and the use of **essential oils** can help to align the chakra. Common applications are in personal care products such as soaps, lotions and sprays Oil diffusers and candles are also great options for introducing beautiful scent into your personal space.

ॐ We all run on solar power! The **sun** is nature's battery! Sunshine contains the complete spectrum of all the colors so it recharges all your chakra simultaneously. This acts as an instantaneous boost even when outdoors for just a few minutes!

ॐ **Exercise** is a great way to move energy throughout the body and unblock your chakra! The practice of yoga was designed to move *prana* (energy) throughout the body with specific *asanas* (poses) using *pranayama* (breathing) techniques. Qigong and Tai Chi are other Eastern meditative practices specifically created with the intention of moving life force energy throughout the body.

ॐ **Sound** provides instantaneous vibrational change making it one of the most powerful tools for your chakra. When in perfect alignment, each chakra will resonate to a certain frequency and note. In a funky mood? Think about how quickly listening to your favorite song, nature sounds or a comedy routine can shift your energy!

ॐ Many forms of **meditation** can be very useful in helping to balance the chakra. Often guided meditations will focus on going through each chakra and visualizing it glowing its specific color and spinning in the proper direction.

🕉 A **mantra** is a sacred word or phrase spoken in repetition used to achieve a consistent state during meditation. Ancient mantras were created to resonate to a sacred vibration that aided in mediation.

🕉 **Affirmations** are positive statements that are used to reinforce an idea or concept. Using affirmative statements is a great way to encourage positive behaviors and actions related to each chakra.

🕉 A **professional** such as a Reiki practitioner or Energy/Light worker can also help you to move energy throughout your body. There are some individuals like myself who can physically see energy and the blockages in order to identify them and help to remove them from the energy body.

CHAKRA 101

Okay, so really, what's the deal with chakras? Most people have heard of the word *chakra* in yoga class or have seen it somewhere, but really don't have an idea of what the chakras are and the impact that they have on the physical body. Chakras act as a part of the subtle energy (non-physical) body and serve as the connection portals from the energy body to specific spots on physical body. Think of a chakra like a faucet, if the chakra is obstructed, it can impede the flow of energy causing blockages and lead to decreased or even no chakra function at all. Pain, discomfort and dis-ease in the physical body are often found where energy is blocked or stagnant in the energetic body. Allowing life force energy to properly flow throughout and around our bodies is what keeps us alive and healthy. This is the same energy that flows throughout every living plant, animal and being in our Universe.

This mystical life force energy that keeps us alive is known by many names, throughout many ancient belief systems: *prana* in Sanskrit, *chi* or *qi* in Chinese and *ki* in the Japanese tradition. The word chakra actually translates to "wheel" or "disk" in Sanskrit, referring to their appearance being similar to that of an energetic spinning vortex. Chakras were first described thousands of years ago in the Hindu books of knowledge, the Vedas, but were only brought to the attention of Western audiences within the past century. Traditional texts indicate that there may be over 88,000 spinning energy nodes or points across the human body connecting the energetic body to the physical body. When discussing the chakras, I will be referencing the seven major chakra points that align with the spine on the physical body (unless otherwise noted). It should be noted that there are approximately 40 secondary chakras that hold special significance and are often referenced in healing work. These chakras are located above, below and on certain parts of the body including the hands and feet. The first three chakras that we will be discussing are the root, sacral, solar plexus chakras, those relating to physical matter or the body. The fourth chakra, the heart chakra, acts as a bridge connecting the physical and the spiritual chakras. The upper three chakras (throat, third eye, crown) are connected to Spirit. (See image on page 10)

Each of the seven main chakras connects to a specific level of the person's energy field or energy body. In esoteric studies, the energy field is often referred to as the aura. The aura is actually the electromagnetic field of energy that surrounds all living beings. This measurable energy field can extend four to five feet beyond the physical being. Much as there are circulatory systems in the body (lymphatic, blood/veins/arteries, etc.), there are circulatory systems in the energetic body called meridians. Meridians are most commonly recognized from the practice of acupuncture, where needles are placed along the body's meridians to help unblock energy.

Imagine this: you're driving down the highway, truckin' along, jammin' out to your favorite music, wind in your hair and all of a sudden you come cruising around a blind corner to see traffic slowing down, stopping you dead in your tracks. That's what happens when a chakra is blocked - the energy in your body cannot move and you get caught in an energetic traffic jam somewhere in the body. When a chakra is open and spinning at the proper rate, at the correct frequency, energy is able to move freely connecting the energetic and physical bodies. This creates an opportunity for an individual to come into alignment being in tune with their higher self, honoring their mind, body and spirit. Though all the chakras function separately, they are able to operate at their full potential when they are all working cohesively.

Bringing awareness to how energy flows is paramount in understanding how to keep the chakras functioning; and how to keep your body, mind and spirit feeling nourished. With each breath you inhale, you welcome life force energy into your body, allowing it to flourish throughout your being. This breath is what nourishes and sustains us, bringing in this beautiful prana. Maintaining your energy is something to be especially conscious of, as the energy throughout your body is constantly fluctuating with each and every breath. The energy around you can affect your chakra, so it is of the utmost importance to be aware of the energies you choose to surround yourself with. Have you ever noticed how flipping channels on the television instantly changes the energy of the room? The news feels heavy, dense and generally icky to me. However, nature shows with cuddly, baby animals feel full of love and good energy. Your energy can be affected by a situation, a place, an emotional upset, or even due to resistance to change. Has your stomach ever cramped up before a meeting with you boss? Your solar plexus, center of personal power, likely became tense. Ever been nervous about a conversation and gotten a sore, scratchy throat? That was your body telling you that your throat chakra was not in alignment. As soon as we are able to bring awareness to a situation we can shift the energy surrounding it.

Here are some potential benefits that may occur when you start to address your own energy via the chakra system:

ॐ Overall improvement in well-being

ॐ Alleviate physical, mental and emotional suffering

ॐ A renewed sense of authentic self-awareness

ॐ Improved relationships (with others and self)

ॐ Conscious communication

ॐ Joyful self-care

ॐ A sense of ease, safety, joy, trust and peace

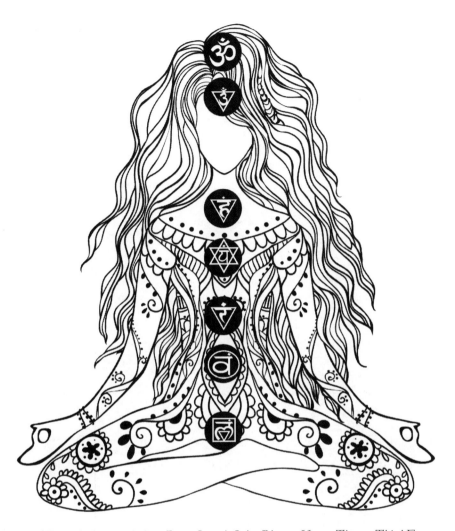

From the bottom chakra: Root, Sacral, Solar Plexus, Heart, Throat, Third Eye, Crown

IS YOUR ROOT CHAKRA BALANCED?

- ॐ Are you lacking focus?
- ॐ Are you co-dependent on another person (or habit)?
- ॐ Are you feeling restless?
- ॐ Are you feeling disconnected from the physical world?
- ॐ Are you more concerned with finances than usual?
- ॐ Are you constipated?
- ॐ Do you feel disconnected from friends and loved ones?
- ॐ Do you feel abandoned?
- ॐ Do you experience sciatic pain?
- ॐ Do you experience leg cramps or muscle spasms?
- ॐ Do you have swelling in your lower limbs?
- ॐ Do you have circulatory issues?

If you answered "yes" to any of these questions, you may have a root chakra imbalance. Over the next few pages, you will learn more about *Muladhara*, the root chakra, its significance and what you can do to help bring it back into perfection.

MULADHARA | I AM

Color	**Red**
Element	**Earth**
Ruled By	**Saturn**
Gemstones	**Hematite, Black Tourmaline, Red Jasper, Garnet, Ruby, Bloodstone, Onyx, Tiger's Eye, Obsidian**
Essential Oils	**Ylang ylang, Cedar Atlas, Juniper, Vetiver, Cinnamon, Patchouli, Spikenard, Nutmeg, Ginger, Myrrh**
Note/Frequency	**C / 7.8 Hz**
Mantra	**Lam**

Muladhara is the word for "support" in Sanskrit. It is considered the root or foundation of the energy body. It is located near the base of the spine, specifically, the first three vertebrae near the coccyx. When this chakra is open and balanced, there is a sense of safety and fearlessness. Once this chakra is operating at its full potential, benefits include feeling centered, fully alive and healthy. People will often feel "down to Earth" and grounded since this chakra connects us to the Earth and Mother Nature.

The main function of this chakra is survival. The root chakra grounds us into the Earth providing a stable base for the rest of the chakra system to build upon. This chakra provides structure to the rest of the system, and if it is not functioning properly, it cannot provide a stable base, impacting the rest of the chakras. The concept of structure often carries into the idea of survival and what we need to do to feel safe and secure. Family, community and tribe have a strong impact on the idea of survival and what we need to feel safe. Often times individuals with who have experienced childhood trauma or have had issues with their parents, experience difficulties with this chakra. This chakra can also be imbalanced as a result of a codependent relationship. People who are in the process of a breakup or a divorce, may also be prone to root chakra imbalances as their concept of family is in transition. An increased concern regarding money and finances may be connected to the idea of survival.

If the chakra is overactive, it can look like impulsiveness or recklessness, even leading to physical aggression. People can also feel hyper active, hyper sexual and may act greedy or egotistical. Feelings of fear, dread and paranoia are also related to this chakra being overactive.

When this chakra is under active, it can manifest as manipulative or possessive behavior. Symptoms can include feeling overly tired, weak, and hopeless. People can feel uninspired, unfocused, unloved and experience a lack in confidence. It can be hard to start the day and fear can often take over emotions. When your root chakra is not balanced, there is often a fear of abandonment.

If an individual has consistent problems with their root chakra, this issue can manifest as obesity. The location of this chakra can also affect the bladder and the colon. Problems with this chakra can also manifest in the legs, often looking like pain and swelling in the legs, feet and ankles.

I feel like this is one of the most important chakras to keep in check and of course one of the chakras that I have had the most issues keeping balanced! When my root chakra is not in balance, my entire body feels "off", almost as if the rest of my body is short circuiting energy and not firing on the proper cylinders. Growing up, I was completely ungrounded and it showed in my inability to control my energy. I would constantly have issues with short circuiting electronics, blowing out light bulbs, and even street lamps as I passed them. The energy flowing through me was almost dangerous when ungrounded. At times the repercussions were my own— breaking the best Hannuakah gift ever after an hour of playing Sonic the Hedgehog was crushing (RIP handheld Sega Genesis). Other times, the consequences were more dire and affected the entire household. For instance, that one time I was angry about something and tearing through my kitchen stress eating, placed a bag of popcorn in the microwave and not even a minute into the cycle, the microwave stopped working. I didn't get the popcorn popped and lets just say my parents were less than thrilled. The microwave didn't get fixed for years—it was part of a built in cabinet that required complete disassembly in order to be fixed. That's just one of the numerous stories I could tell you about how my lack of energetic control affected those around me, but you haven't got eternity to sit there reading.

My imbalanced root chakra affected me far greater than it affected anyone else, however. As a baby, my family had nicknamed me "Buddha" as a result of my smiley face and never ending cascade of fat rolls. One of those stuck, and not the one I would have hoped for. I was always overweight; I had never really grown out of that baby fat phase. This was not due to poor diet or lack of exercise, actually just the opposite, my Mom and step Dad were extremely health conscious and provided strict regiments to try and help me slim down. Still, I remained overweight, no one truly understanding that the mass I was holding around my middle was not weight, but energy. This was energy that I was using to protect myself; to act as a barrier between myself and the world. At that time, I didn't understand my own energy, so my body instinctively did what it had to do to try and protect itself. Once I fully understood that if I maintained my energy properly, my body wouldn't have to protect itself, the excess weight started dropping off.

A great place to start balancing out the root chakra is by eating grounding food, for example, root vegetables such as beets, turnips, parsnips, radishes and potatoes. Foods that grow deep in the earth are good for nourishing our root chakra. There are a number of spices that also grow as roots including turmeric, ginseng, and ginger. Since the root chakra vibrates on a red frequency, naturally red foods are a great option to keep up the chakra's energy. This chakra controls including immune, skeletal and adrenal functions which are supported by red foods, as they often high in vitamin C.

Anything with protein is also considered grounding food as well: eggs, beans, as well as animal based protein. Energy is able to move easiest through natural, unprocessed food, as it is of the earth, our bodies are intended to consume it. If you do choose to consume animal based protein, it is important to be conscientious of the conditions it was raised in, what it was fed and the overall manner in which it has been presented (organic, Kosher, etc.). All of these are factors in the energy it will carry, and thus what you will consume into your energy when you eat it. Myself, when I choose to consume animal proteins, I tend to stick with lighter options like seafood and poultry. To me, these feel like they have a lighter density and do not leave me feeling heavy and blocked after consumption. That being said, there are. times when you just want a cheeseburger and nothing else can satisfy that craving. I would just make sure it's a really damn good cheeseburger, and not some cheap fast food.

Being outside in nature is one of my favorite ways to balance this chakra. Sometimes that is as simple as going outside with bare feet and feeling the Earth beneath me, supporting and grounding me. Other days, I am drawn to leave my surroundings and immerse myself in Mother Nature's beauty, retreating to the mountains or the forest. I have also been known to go outside and hug a tree. Any connection with Earth energy is cleansing and grounding. Holding crystals is another one of my favorite ways to ground, especially if I am unable to get outside to due to inclement weather.

During the next three days, you will be focusing on your roots and who you are at your core. Wearing red clothing, red jewelry and eating naturally red foods are a great way to flood this chakra with extra energy as you are cleansing and clearing it. Drinking chai, cinnamon or dandelion root tea as a way to help ground yourself as well.

<u>Day One:</u> Who are you at your root? Think of 10 things about **YOU** that resonate the most with who you are at your core and finish the statements below.

I am _____

I am _____

I am _____

I am _____

I am _____

I am _____

I am _____

I am _____

I am _____

I am _____

Did your list look like you thought it would when you started? Were there any surprises that came up when thinking about who you really are? Did you struggle to complete this list? Take some time to contemplate your responses and what they mean in leading a fulfilling life.

Day Two: Take some time to connect with the Earth today and ground yourself into her energy. This can be done through an activity like gardening, taking a walk or sitting outside having a picnic. Try putting your bare feet on the ground and envision roots sprouting from your feet grounding you into the Earth. Allow the Earth's energy to envelop you, transmuting any feelings of fear and lack into love and abundance. How did it feel to get grounded? Reflect on your experience.

_____

_____

_____

_____

_____

_____

_____

_____

_____

_____

_____

_____

_____

_____

_____

_____

_____

_____

_____

<u>Day Three:</u> Who am I at my core? What grounds me? Do I feel supported? Reflect on these questions and your observations from the past three days of focus on your root chakra.

_____

_____

_____

_____

_____

_____

_____

_____

_____

_____

_____

_____

_____

_____

_____

_____

_____

_____

_____

_____

_____

_____

_____

_____

_____

_____

_____

_____

_____

_____

_____

_____

_____

_____

_____

_____

_____

_____

_____

_____

_____

_____

_____

Take a look back at the questions listed in the beginning of the chapter. When you ask yourself the questions, are your answers still the same as they were the three days ago?

IS YOUR SACRAL CHAKRA BALANCED?

🕉 Are you depressed?

🕉 Are you impotent?

🕉 Are you overly jealous?

🕉 Are you struggling with fertility?

🕉 Are you unable to achieve orgasm?

🕉 Do you experience low self-esteem?

🕉 Do you experience lower back pain?

🕉 Do you experience unexplained fear?

🕉 Do you find yourself in unhealthy relationships?

🕉 Do you have a hard time getting close to people, even loved ones?

🕉 Do you have abnormal menstruation or other related issues?

🕉 Do you suffer from frequent UTIs and/or kidney infections?

If you answered "yes" to any of these questions, you may have a sacral chakra imbalance. Over the next few pages, you will learn more about *Svadhisthana*, the sacral chakra, its significance and what you can do to help bring it back into perfection.

SVADHISTHANA | I FEEL

Color	Orange
Element	Water
Ruled By	Moon
Gemstones	Carnelian, Rutilated Quartz, Amber, Citrine, Orange Calcite
Essential Oils	Mandarin Red, Patchouli, Bergamot, Clary Sage, Sweet Orange, Tangerine, Geranium, Texas Cedarwood, Neroli
Note/Frequency	D / 15.6 Hz
Mantra	Vam

The second chakra, Svadhisthana, means "sweetness" in Sanskrit. This chakra is connected to the movement and flow of emotions and relationships. Sensuality is an important aspect of this chakra as well, as is nurturing, warmth and touch. The main functions of this chakra are pleasure, desire and (pro)creation. It is located between the pubic bone and the navel, meaning its location can impact the kidneys, genitals and womb.

When this chakra is open and operating at the proper frequency, there is a high quality and quantity of love, mentally, physically and spiritually. Every part of your being feels good; you nurture your mind and body, while appreciating the physical world that surrounds you. Creativity and imagination are optimized through intuition. Balancing this chakra can creates a sense of belongingness, improves concern for others and overall shifts appreciation and depth of relationships.

If this chakra is overactive, this can manifest as selfish, arrogant and power-seeking behaviors. An individual can act overly proud or be on a constant pursuit of pleasure moving forward without a plan or taking responsibility for their actions. This can also manifest as an over active sex drive and in extreme cases, addiction to sex and pornography.

An under active sacral chakra may result in the inability to express emotions, strong judgment of others, and can be coupled with mistrustful, antisocial behavior. People will often feel constricted by moral codes and be clouded with righteous ideals of good and bad. There is often a desire to be a perfectionist and control the surrounding environment. This can manifest as issues with sex including lack of arousal, or inability to reach orgasm. Consistent blockages in the second chakra can manifest as bladder or kidney problems.

Through working with clients who have had traumatic sexual experiences or have been sexually abused, I have observed that there is often residual issues with this chakra. As a clairvoyant, I will often see this chakra looking broken or shattered. In these cases, I often opt to completely replace the broken portal, transmuting any old energy to the light and bringing in a fresh, new chakra. This allows for more consistent energy flow and aids in releasing emotions related to past traumas.

As a child, it was very challenging for me to hold relationships. I didn't have many friends and I didn't know how to express myself. Being around too many other people in school was overwhelming and emotionally taxing. I would need time after school to decompress from all the energy of the other kids. I normally only had one or two close friends until I would inevitably sabotage the relationship after getting "too close". At the time, I had no idea that my lack of emotional resonance stemmed from my lack of boundaries, energetic control and imbalanced chakras. As an adult, I was repeatedly faced with the same repetitious patterns of these destructive relationships, each one becoming obvious than the last as they imploded. When I stopped to take a look, I realized that all of the problems that I had with others in my life were reflections of my own issues. I had to get my own energy and emotions in check before I could maintain any semblance of a normal, healthy relationship with anyone else.

As this chakra is ruled by the element of water, liquids are one of the best ways help to balance out the sacral chakra. A sacred soak in the bathtub with rose petals and essential oils speaks directly to this chakra. A moonlight swim in a pool or a natural body of water can be very spiritually cleansing as well. Water symbolizes emotions in metaphysical studies, so use this knowledge as an additional tool to really cleanse yourself of what is holding you back emotionally. Envision the water washing away anything that is no longer serving your highest and best good.

Naturally orange foods such as pumpkin and apricots help to balance this chakra. Healthy fats including oils, nuts and seeds also resonate on a similar vibration, providing support to the organs surrounding this chakra. Given the location of the sacral chakra, the foods that nourish this chakra provides for optimal reproductive and urinary tract health. As fermented foods are technically still living they are also connected to this chakra. Fish that are high in healthy fats are excellent high protein options for this chakra as well.

During the next three days, you will be focusing on your feelings and relationship with the world around you. Wearing orange clothing, orange jewelry and eating naturally orange foods are a great way to flood this chakra with extra energy as you are cleansing and clearing it. Drinking lots of water and other liquids will aid in the balancing of your sacral chakra.

<u>Day Four:</u> The sacral chakra controls how you feel, in mind, body and spirit. What do you feel? Think about 10 things that you resonate strongly with and finish the phrases below.

I feel _____

I feel _____

I feel _____

I feel _____

I feel _____

I feel _____

I feel _____

I feel _____

I feel _____

I feel _____

Did your list look like you thought it would when you started? Were there any surprises that came up when thinking about what you actually feel? Did you struggle to complete this list? Take some time to contemplate your responses and what they mean to you in terms of how you process feelings and emotions.

Day Five: Dancing is one of my favorite ways to balance the sacral chakra. Spend at least five minutes today moving around to your favorite beat. The movement of your hips works to open up the sacral chakra. When was the last time you allowed yourself to experience the sheer joy that comes with dancing to your favorite music at full blast?

Journal: What brings me sheer joy? How can I fit that into my daily routine? Reflect on these questions and todays activity.

_____

_____

_____

_____

_____

_____

_____

_____

_____

_____

_____

_____

_____

_____

_____

_____

_____

_____

_____

_____

<u>Day Six:</u> Am I moving through my emotions and desires in healthy and productive manner? Am I allowing myself to feel pleasure? Express my sensuality? Creativity? Reflect on these questions and your observations from the past three days of focus on your sacral chakra.

_____

_____

_____

_____

_____

_____

_____

_____

_____

_____

_____

_____

_____

_____

_____

_____

_____

_____

_____

_____

_____

_____

_____

_____

_____

_____

_____

_____

_____

_____

_____

_____

_____

_____

_____

_____

_____

_____

_____

_____

Take a look back at the questions listed in the beginning of the chapter. When you ask yourself the questions, are your answers still the same as they were the three days ago?

IS YOUR SOLAR PLEXUS CHAKRA BALANCED?

ॐ Are you a perfectionist?

ॐ Are you anxious?

ॐ Are you controlling?

ॐ Do you carry excess weight around your middle section?

ॐ Do you have any addictions?

ॐ Do you have poor digestion, gas or nausea on a regular basis?

ॐ Do you have trouble losing, gaining or maintaining weight?

ॐ Do you have ulcers?

ॐ Do you lack courage?

ॐ Do you lack self-control?

ॐ Do you struggle to maintain healthy boundaries?

ॐ Do you seek the approval of others before your own?

If you answered "yes" to any of these questions, you may have a solar plexus chakra imbalance. Over the next few pages, you will learn more about *Manipura*, the solar plexus chakra, its significance and what you can do to help bring it back into perfection.

MANIPURA | I ACT

Color	Yellow
Element	Fire
Ruled By	Mars
Gemstones	Citrine, Golden Calcite, Golden Topaz, Sunstone
Essential Oil	Rosemary, Lemon, Grapefruit, Bergamot, Balsam Fir Needle, Clove, Coriander, Lemongrass
Note/Frequency	E / 22.4 Hz
Mantra	Ram

The third chakra, Manipura, means "lustrous gem" referring to the center of personal power and free will. More commonly referred to by its location near the solar plexus, it is located from the navel to just beneath the breastbone. This chakra supports the concepts of belonging, transformation and self-esteem. Balance, will and determination are also ideas connected to the solar plexus.

The main function of this chakra is willpower. When this chakra is open and operating in perfection, there is a higher quality and quantity of love in every aspect of life: mentally, physically and spiritually. There is a sense of personal pride and nurturing the body from head to toe when this is in harmony. Individuals are able to take the time to enjoy their physical surroundings. People are friendly, feel a sense of belongingness and show a concern for others. The sense of humor is thought to come from this chakra as well.

When this chakra is open, there is a strong sense of belonging and being firmly grounded in the universe. If this chakra is closed, feelings may be blocked, and it can be difficult to understand the deeper meanings of emotions. There is often difficulty when connecting to a greater life purpose. If this chakra is over active it can manifest as selfish, arrogant or power seeking behaviors. People can act overly proud or be on a relentless pursuit of pleasure without concern of any responsibility for their actions. There are often lofty visions with no action plans. When this chakra is over active, people are often anti-social or "followers", unable to express their emotions, and restricted by moral codes. These people will often see the future as clouded with righteous ideals of good and bad. If this chakra is under active it can look like mistrustful, perfectionist or judgmental behaviors. People who consider themselves to be "control freaks" often struggle with this chakra. The location of this chakra can have long term affects on the panaceas, the adrenals and the digestive system. Ulcers, diabetes, and hypoglycemia can appear as manifestations of long term issues with this chakra.

I have always had stomach problems. As a child, it was not uncommon for me to spend hours in the bathroom. We knew that I had food allergies, but no one really could grasp what was causing the intense cramping and sharp pains. Doctors would tell me that I needed to lower fat intake over gallbladder concerns or that I had IBS (Irritable Bowel Syndrome), but years went by without definite answers as to the source of my constant discomfort. My stomach problems wouldn't start to subside until I came to the realization that they weren't connected to what I ate as much as what I surrounded myself with. When I didn't have any control over my life, I could physically feel the twisting and the tightness of my solar plexus chakra. As I took back control of my career, my relationships and my life, the stress I held in my stomach subsided and the pain started to dwindle.

This chakra is ruled by the element of fire and we can use that knowledge in a number of applications. Fire traditionally symbolizes passion and creativity, but to me it has always been more representative of cleansing and purification. A great way to use fire to cleanse this chakra is to write a letter(s) to anyone who you hold anger or resentment against and then burn the letter. By writing a letter, you are expressing your truth in a safe space. The fire transmutes anything that is no longer serving you allowing you to take back your personal power. Warming spices such as pepper, cinnamon and ginger help to keep the chakra operating in perfection. Essential oils derived from warming spices are often used in beauty applications to promote healthy circulation. When eaten warming spices are said to increase the metabolism, which is one of the body's natural purification systems. Detox baths with fresh ginger root are a great way to cleanse the body from the inside out.

Food is a great way to address concerns with the solar plexus chakra, especially given its proximity to the stomach and digestive system. Of course, any naturally yellow colored foods and spices work in harmony to balance this chakra, but there are other beneficial foods for this chakra as well. Anything that is beneficial for the digestive system is valuable to the solar plexus chakra, including whole grains and legumes as they promote good digestive health. Natural sweeteners (in moderation, as with everything) are also connected to this chakra.

Over the next three days, you will be focusing on your feelings of power in relationship to the world around you. Wearing yellow clothing, yellow jewelry and eating naturally yellow foods are a great way to flood this chakra with extra energy as you are cleansing and clearing it. Getting some extra sunshine will aid in the balancing of your solar plexus chakra.

<u>Day Seven:</u> Manipura, the solar plexus chakra, is the core of your personal power and free will. Does how you act resonate with your true self? Think about 10 things relating to how you act and finish the phrases below.

I act _____

I act _____

I act _____

I act _____

I act _____

I act _____

I act _____

I act _____

I act _____

I act _____

Did your list look like you thought it would when you started? Were there any surprises that came up when thinking about how you act? Did you struggle to complete this list? Take some time to contemplate your responses and what they mean in regards to your actions and motivating factors when moving through how you (re)act to life around you every day.

<u>Day Eight:</u> Often times we do things that do not serve our highest and best good, purely out of a sense of obligation to others. The only obligation that we truly hold is to ourselves. After all, we cannot help others if we are not taking care of ourselves first. Think about 10 things that you do that are no longer serving you and list them below.

1. _____

2. _____

3. _____

4. _____

5. _____

6. _____

7. _____

8. _____

9. _____

10. _____

Are you ready to start honoring yourself? Take a deep breath in and exhale, letting go of anything that no longer serves you. Often times awareness is enough to change the energy of the situation and allow you to move forward into healing.

<u>Day Nine:</u> Am I in control of my personal power and will? Am I acting authentically with my best interests being considered first? Reflect on these questions and your observations from the past three days of focus on your solar plexus chakra.

_____

_____

_____

_____

_____

_____

_____

_____

_____

_____

_____

_____

_____

_____

_____

_____

_____

_____

_____

_____

_____

_____

Take a look back at the questions listed in the beginning of the chapter. When you ask yourself the questions, are your answers still the same as they were the three days ago?

IS YOUR HEART CHAKRA BALANCED?

ॐ Are you overly critical towards yourself or others?

ॐ Are you shy?

ॐ Do you experience respiratory problems such as asthma?

ॐ Do you feel lonely?

ॐ Do you feel rejected?

ॐ Do you feel unloved or unlovable?

ॐ Do you find it hard to accept compliments?

ॐ Do you have heart problems?

ॐ Do you lack empathy?

ॐ Do you struggle to acknowledge and/or express your emotions?

ॐ Is change difficult for you?

ॐ Is there someone you have not forgiven?

If you answered "yes" to any of these questions, you may have a heart chakra imbalance. Over the next few pages, you will learn more about *Anahata*, the heart chakra, its significance and what you can do to help bring it back into perfection.

ANAHATA | I LOVE

Color	Green (physical), Pink (spiritual)
Element	Air
Ruled By	Venus
Gemstones	Rose Quartz, Watermelon Tourmaline, Rhodonite, Amazonite, Emerald, Chrysocolla, Malachite, Morganite, Peridot, Moss Agate, Green Adventurine, Green Calcite, Green Flourite
Essential Oils	Eucalyptus, Pine, Spearmint, Rose
Note/Frequency	F / 30.2 Hz
Mantra	Yam

The fourth chakra, Anahata, means "unhurt, unstuck or unbeaten" in Sanskrit. This speaks to the resilience of the heart and our innate capacity for unconditional love. The heart chakra connects the physical chakra (root, sacral and solar plexus) to the spiritual chakra (throat, third eye and crown). In doing so, this chakra becomes the bridge between the mind, body, spirit, bringing the emotions and the center of the energy body. The color pink nourishes the spiritual aspect of the heart chakra, while the color green encourages the physical healing of this chakra. The main function of this chakra is love. This love is not the love of need or desire, it is the joyous acceptance of our place at this time. This is the understanding that the Universe has everything provided for us, and we will have whatever we need, in the proper time.

When this chakra is open and balanced, life is good. You are living out your purpose, enjoying what you are doing. You experience harmony, generosity and love. Understanding, adaptability and compassion are second nature. Friendly, humanitarian acts come from this place of pure joy. You are able to see the good in everyone. If this chakra is overactive, it can result in jealous, moody and over confident behavior. It can also manifest as angry, demanding, possessive and overly critical actions. When this chakra is under active, people often feel unloved, sorry for themselves, and are afraid of being alone or abandoned. Under activity here can appear as a lack of compassion, paranoia, or general indecisiveness. People struggling to keep this chakra in balance will constantly need external reminders of their self worth. Problems with this chakra can manifest into heart problems such as high blood pressure or heart disease. Proximity to the chest and lung regions means that it can also manifest as asthma, lung disease and other respiratory illnesses.

This is the chakra that I have had to do the most work on. Sensitive was truly an understatement, everything in my periphery affected me in some way. Watching historical documentaries, television shows or movies that contained any upsetting or graphic images was physically painful and deeply frightening. It hurt my heart to watch the pain and suffering of others to the point of physically manifesting pain. Hospitals and medical facilities were overwhelming to the point of panic attacks, shallow breathing and heart palpitations. I could feel the agony and discomfort of the patients so deeply that I could not focus or even stay in my body. This chakra imbalance also manifested when I would see people who were truly happy and in love. It physically pained me to see this because my heart space was so closed off. I never saw myself as fit to love or be loved, so it was confusing when I saw it and hurtful when I wasn't able to feel it or truly experience it myself. At this point, I have learned to channel such deep awareness into a blessing with the type of work I do.

This chakra is represented by the element of air. The most pure application of this idea is to be outside in nature, able to breathe in fresh air. There is no coincidence that green chakra connects us to nature and reminds us the importance of the overall health of the mind, body and spirit. As this chakra is connected to air, breathing is also of the utmost importance, making yoga a great way to incorporate additional heart healing.

Since green represents the physical aspects of the heart chakra, it is no wonder that the most beneficial foods for this chakra are dark, leafy greens. Thinking outside the box on how to add in extra green to your meals is easy once you get the hang of it! Try adding a handful of spinach into your morning smoothie, or having a veggie omelet for breakfast. Oven baked kale chips are a great snack for the afternoon! There are tons of ways to get in your greens aside from salads and wheat grass shots, I promise! (Unless that's your jam, wheat grass away!)

Over the course of the next three days, you will be focusing on your feelings relating to love. Wearing green or pink clothing, green or pink jewelry and eating naturally green foods are a great way to flood this chakra with extra energy as you are cleansing and clearing it. Getting some extra hugs and healthy forms of affection will aid in the balancing of your heart chakra.

Day Ten: Anahata, the heart chakra, is concerned with all things relating to love. Think about 10 things that you love and finish the phrases below.

I love _____

I love _____

I love _____

I love _____

I love _____

I love _____

I love _____

I love _____

I love _____

I love _____

Did your list look like you thought it would when you started? Were there any surprises that came up when thinking about who, what, where, when, how and why you love? Did you struggle to complete this list? Take some time to contemplate your responses and what they mean in regards to how you address love in your life.

Day Eleven: Try a Metta mediation today to encourage loving kindness. Metta means "kindness, benevolence, and goodwill" in Pali, the sacred language of Theravada Buddhism. Start by first focusing on loving yourself. Encase yourself in a beautiful bubble of pink love, then slowly expanding your love bubble to include a good friend, then follow with a neutral individual. Next include a difficult person in your life in your love bubble, then all of the above equally. Finally, include the entire universe in your love. Reflect on your experience below.

Day Twelve: Is there appropriate balance between the giving and receiving of love and compassion, both for myself and for others? Reflect on this question and your observations from the past three days of focus on your heart chakra.

_____

_____

_____

_____

_____

_____

_____

_____

_____

_____

_____

_____

_____

_____

_____

_____

_____

_____

_____

_____

_____

_____

_____

_____

_____

_____

_____

_____

_____

_____

_____

_____

_____

_____

_____

_____

_____

_____

_____

Take a look back at the questions listed in the beginning of the chapter. When you ask yourself the questions, are your answers still the same as they were the three days ago?

IS YOUR THROAT CHAKRA BALANCED?

ॐ   Are you feeling unheard?

ॐ   Are you keeping secrets from loved ones?

ॐ   Do you experience allergies?

ॐ   Do you feel misunderstood?

ॐ   Do you have a fear of public speaking?

ॐ   Do you have frequent sore throats?

ॐ   Do you have neck pain?

ॐ   Do you have thyroid problems?

ॐ   Do you say one thing but feel another?

ॐ   Do you suffer from TMJ?

ॐ   Do you tell people what they want to hear?

ॐ   Is it hard to express your truth?

If you answered "yes" to any of these questions, you may have a throat chakra imbalance. Over the next few pages, you will learn more about *Visuddha*, the throat chakra, its significance and what you can do to help bring it back into perfection.

VISUDDHA | I SPEAK

Color	**Blue**
Element	**Sound**
Ruled By	**Mercury**
Gemstones	**Sodalite, Lapis Lazuli, Azurite, Blue Lace Agate, Angelite, Celestite, Blue Calcite, Blue Quartz, Blue Sapphire, Kyanite, Larimar, Turquoise**
Essential Oils	**Geranium, Chamomile, Peppermint, Cypress, Spearmint**
Note/Frequency	**G / 38.0 Hz**
Mantra	**Ham**

The fifth chakra, Visuddha, means "purification". The idea of purification has always represented shedding the things that are no longer in alignment with my highest good in my experiences. Communication, creativity and speaking your highest truths are all related to this chakra. This chakra is located at the base of the throat and can be associated with pain in the neck, shoulders, arms and hands. It can also affect the areas above it including the jaw, mouth and tongue as these are directly connected to verbal communication. The throat chakra is represented by the element of sound which aligns perfectly with the idea of speaking your truth.

When this chakra is open and balanced, people are good speakers, often musically and artistically inclined, and are able to live in the present moment. There is a good sense of timing, inventiveness and tactfulness. Peace, affection and relaxation are not only attainable, but the status quo. People who have a balanced throat chakra are loyal, centered and faithful. Communication is purposeful. Individuals are able to tune into high thought vibrations that serve a positive purpose.

When this chakra is overactive, it can look like fanatical, hyperactive, and even domineering behaviors. People can act arrogant, self-righteous, and dogmatic. Feelings can be overwhelming and too complicated to simplify. If this chakra is under active, it can manifest as stubborn, scared, timid or quiet behaviors. It can be hard to accept change, people may feel negative and confusing thoughts that are not in alignment with the their inner truth. People feel generally unreliable and weak. In some extreme cases, behavior can be devious and manipulative. Addictive behaviors may also be connected to this chakra and not speaking your highest truth in regards to wants, needs and desires. Long term problems with this chakra can manifest as sore throats, stiff neck, colds, thyroid problems, and hearing problems.

Growing up I constantly had sore throats, leading to the removal of my tonsils and adenoids in high school. We could never figure out why I had constant problems in this area. I did my best to take care of my throat as a fledgling singer, it was of the utmost importance to me, but nearly every other week I struggled with this area. Now over ten years later, I can look back and clearly see that these ailments were directly connected to the lack of personal truth that I was expressing. I wasn't comfortable in myself, my skills or speaking up for what I wanted or needed. This created years of discomfort and severe pain that stopped me from delivering my truth.

Exercising your throat chakra and learning to clear it is maybe one of the best things that you can learn to do for yourself. This can come through many different forms of expression. Writing always gave me a voice when mine couldn't be heard. Different kinds of writing such as journaling, poetry or song writing can allow for different aspects of self to be healed. Painting can also be a therapeutic outlet for this chakra, expressing truth via artwork. Singing is another great form of verbal communication that allows energy to move. Nothing beats singing (or cry-sobbing) at the top of your lungs to a love song, when you are going through a tough break up, right?

I will often joke that swearing is a form of cleansing this chakra as well. This brings up fond memories of my grandmother who was what we in our family would refer to as a "closet swearer". She picked up her mouth from her mother, but only let it out while surrounded by friends and loved ones. It was hysterical to hear her drop an f-bomb and quickly try and cover for swearing in front of her grandkids. She was a woman who always spoke her truth, no matter what and I tend to think that her frequent use of colorful language helped make that possible. Thanks for the reminder, Barbara.

As this chakra is more of a spiritual chakra than a physical chakra, the use of food as a balancing agent is less prevalent. There are very few naturally blue foods, but this chakra can be balanced with water and other nutrient-rich liquids. Foods that fall off the tree when they are ripe and ready and requiring little to no work in order to be enjoyed are also said to balance this chakra. These fruits include apples, pears, peaches, apricots, and plums.

During the next three days, you will be focusing on communication. Wearing blue clothing, blue jewelry and eating foods that support this chakra are great way to flood it with extra energy as you are cleansing and clearing it. Listening to your favorite music or soundscape will aid in the balancing of your throat chakra.

<u>Day Thirteen:</u> Visuddha, the throat chakra, controls how you present your truth. Think about 10 things that resonate with you and finish the phrases below.

I speak _____

I speak _____

I speak _____

I speak _____

I speak _____

I speak _____

I speak _____

I speak _____

I speak _____

I speak _____

Did your list look like you thought it would when you started? Were there any surprises that came up when thinking about how you speak? Did you struggle to complete this list? Take some time to contemplate your responses and what they mean in regards to your actions and motivating factors when speaking your trtuh.

Day Fourteen: How aligned are you with your inner truth? Take some time today to do some automatic writing. Ask your higher self what your inner truth is and let your pen do the rest. Don't think about it, just let the ink flow and see what treasures you discover about yourself. There is no right or wrong to this exercise, as long as you try.

Day Fifteen: Am I expressing myself honestly and openly? How do I define healthy communication? Reflect on these questions and your experience over the last three days of focusing on your throat chakra.

_____

_____

_____

_____

_____

_____

_____

_____

_____

_____

_____

_____

_____

_____

_____

_____

_____

_____

_____

_____

_____

_____

_____

_____

_____

_____

_____

_____

_____

_____

_____

_____

_____

_____

_____

_____

_____

_____

_____

_____

_____

Take a look back at the questions listed in the beginning of the chapter. When you ask yourself the questions, are your answers still the same as they were the three days ago?

IS YOUR THIRD EYE CHAKRA BALANCED?

- ॐ Are you depressed?
- ॐ Are you easily confused?
- ॐ Are you frequently sick?
- ॐ Do you experience seizures?
- ॐ Do you experience vivid dreams or nightmares?
- ॐ Do you have a hard time remembering things?
- ॐ Do you have frequent headaches or migraines?
- ॐ Do you have frequent sinus congestion?
- ॐ Do you have hearing problems?
- ॐ Do you have poor vision?
- ॐ Do you suffer from insomnia?
- ॐ Is it hard to understand others?

If you answered "yes" to any of these questions, you may have a third eye chakra imbalance. Over the next few pages, you will learn more about *Ajna*, the third eye chakra, its significance and what you can do to help bring it back into perfection.

AJNA | I SEE

Color	Indigo
Element	Light
Ruled By	Jupiter
Gemstones	Amethyst, Fluorite, Sugilite, Charoite, Lepidolite,
Essential Oils	Frankincense, Myrrh, Patchouli, Bay Laurel, Elemi, Marjoram, Vanilla
Note/Frequency	A / 46.8 Hz
Mantra	Ooo

The sixth chakra, Ajna, means "to know, to perceive or to command" in Sanskrit. Also known as the third eye chakra, the main functions of this chakra are intuition and sight. The third eye is actually the pineal gland which controls the body's sleep patterns and body rhythms. One of the great philosophers, Descartes believed that the pineal gland was the "principal seat of the soul". This chakra is the center of intuition and inner vision along with physical human sight. This chakra is represented by the color indigo and its element is light.

When this chakra is open and balanced, probable events can be seen with clarity. There is a connection to your sense of insight and inner vision. Change and flexibility are welcomed and easy to maintain. There is often a sense of fearlessness, coupled with a desire to fulfill a personal obligation. Clairvoyance and clairsentience, along with all other psychic abilities are optimized.

If this chakra is over active, it can look like impatience, egomania, or authoritarian behaviors. People can also act overly proud or belittle the behavior of others. When too much energy is surging through this chakra, behavior can be highly manipulative. If this chakra is under active, there are strong feelings of self-doubt, envy, and fear. People are often superstitious, overly worried and highly sensitive. Behaviors can be non-assertive or undisciplined as well. Consistent issues with this chakra can manifest as eyestrains, blurred vision, headaches, nightmares, and in extreme cases even blindness.

I have horrible vision with my physical eyes. My friends often refer to the lenses in my glasses as coke bottles and become immediately dizzy when trying them on just "to see how blind I am". I am actually almost legally blind in my right eye. In school, I remember having to ask to sit closer to the front of the classroom because I could not see the blackboard. For years I didn't understand why I suffered with such poor eyesight and eyes that couldn't focus naturally, forcing me to wear corrective lenses in order for me to see with 20/20 vision. What I didn't understand until recently was that this was designed so that I could see clairvoyantly. By not forcing my eyes to focus naturally, this allowed me to see around things, allowing my third eye chakra to develop in order for me to see things that others may not naturally perceive.

Another interesting thing that I perceived as a negative side effect of my poor human vision were the intense glares that I experienced while driving at night. Through a conversation with a friend who has been working to expand her clairvoyance, I came to understand that the stronger the glare and reflection, the deeper my third eye was seeing into the light. I finally understood that this was the blessing, not the curse that I initially assumed it was.

It has always been a challenge for me to fall asleep and then stay asleep for extended periods overnight. Whenever I close my eyes to fall asleep at night, I do not see black. I see the most beautiful, color-filled geometric patterns moving all around, creating the most fantastic electric light show you've ever seen. As gorgeous as it is, this can be quite distracting and frankly overwhelming at times. I have come to the understanding that this is another level of my gifts, providing me a strong connection to the dimensions above when I lay down to sleep.

Deeply colored, purple foods are excellent support for the third eye chakra. As this chakra is more spiritual, there are less foods that support it than the physical chakras. Foods that are high in Omega 3s support healthy brain function and the third eye chakra. High flavonoid foods such as red wine and chocolate should be consumed in moderation.

During the next three days, you will be focusing on your intuition. Wearing indigo clothing, indigo jewelry and eating foods that support this chakra are great way to flood it with extra energy as you are cleansing and clearing it. Meditation is the best way to support the strength of this chakra. By closing your eyes and focusing your attention on your brow, you can become aware of this chakra and all it has to offer.

Day Sixteen: Ajna, the third eye chakra, connects you to your intuition and knowingness. Think about 10 things that you see and finish the phrases below with what resonates for you.

I see _____

I see _____

I see _____

I see _____

I see _____

I see _____

I see _____

I see _____

I see _____

I see _____

Did your list look like you thought it would when you started? Were there any surprises that came up when thinking about what you see? Did you struggle to complete this list? Take some time to contemplate your responses and what they mean in regards to how you see the world around you.

Day Seventeen: Take three small separate pieces of paper (notecard, post-it, etc.) and write down the words "yes", "no" and "maybe". Flip the cards over and mix them around so you don't know which card says what. Ask a question that you know the answer to and place your hand over each card, feeling the difference in the energy of each. Pick the card that you feel the strongest pull towards. Keep practicing for at least five minutes or until you feel more comfortable using your intuition. Reflect on your experience below.

<u>Day Eighteen:</u> Am I trusting my intuition fully? Am I able to discern intuitive guidance form my own thoughts and emotions? Reflect on these questions and the past three days of focus on your third eye chakra.

_____

_____

_____

_____

_____

_____

_____

_____

_____

_____

_____

_____

_____

_____

_____

_____

_____

_____

_____

_____

_____

Take a look back at the questions listed in the beginning of the chapter. When you ask yourself the questions, are your answers still the same as they were the three days ago?

IS YOUR CROWN CHAKRA BALANCED?

ॐ Do you feel isolated?

ॐ Do you lack direction in life?

ॐ Do you feel destructive either towards yourself or others?

ॐ Are you constantly frustrated?

ॐ Do you experience nerve pain?

ॐ Are you experiencing hair loss?

ॐ Do you experience frequent mood swings?

ॐ Do you have any learning challenges?

ॐ Is it hard to set and/or maintain goals?

ॐ Do you have any neurological disorders?

ॐ Are you feeling disconnected spiritually?

ॐ Do you have any psychological conditions?

If you answered "yes" to any of these questions, you may have a crown chakra imbalance. Over the next few pages, you will learn more about *Sahasrara*, the crown chakra, its significance and what you can do to help bring it back into perfection.

SAHASRARA | I UNDERSTAND

Color	**Purple (physical)/White (spiritual)**
Element	**Thought**
Ruled By	**Uranus**
Gemstones	**Clear Quartz, Selenite**
Essential Oil	**Lavender, Helichrysum, Vetiver, Frankincense**
Note/Frequency	**B / 54.6 Hz**
Mantra	**Mmm**

The seventh major chakra, Sahasrara, means "thousand fold" in Sanskrit. This is in reference to the thousand-petal flower that visually represents this chakra. It is located on the top of the head, more commonly known as the crown chakra. This chakra's main function is understanding and helps to facilitate our connection to the Divine. This chakra is representative of enlightenment, and allows for a connection with our higher selves, other beings and the Divine.

When this chakra is open and balanced, there is often great mental strength and immense higher knowledge. Inspiration and kindness are abundant. Enlightenment and connection to Source, are the most celebrated impacts of this chakra function. The proximity to the brain means this chakra can affect the cerebral cortex, central nervous system and pituitary glands. Problems with this chakra can manifest as depression, boredom, apathy, confusion and an inability to learn. People can also feel alienated when there are imbalances in this chakra.

If this chakra is overactive, individuals crave sympathy and have a need to feel indispensable. Behaviors can seem superior, snobbish or arrogant. There is a constant sense of frustration and unrealized power that leads to destructive actions and behaviors. An over active crown chakra can also produce an extremely erotic imagination. When this chakra is under active, there is a sense of shame and negative self image. People are ungrounded and do not feel connected to the Earth. Individuals often feel indecisive, misunderstood, and are stuck in cycles of self-denial. There is no spark of joy to be found.

The crown chakra is directly connected to the pituitary gland. The pituitary gland is known as the master gland since it acts as a main control center that sends messages to all the other glands. The pituitary gland is referred to as the "seat of the mind". The frontal lobe regulates emotional thoughts such as poetry and music, and the anterior lobe regulates concrete thought and intellectual concepts. The pituitary gland is also known as the "fourth eye". When the third eye and the forth eye are in alignment, it is said that the intuition is completely open and activated.

From personal experience, I have learned that most imbalance in this chakra is often related to mental illness or what the public has conditioned to think of as mental illness. When this chakra is open and the person is unaware of their own power, it can be confusing if they have no guidance as to what is going on. I was unaware that I had clairaudient abilities and I began to hear voices and suggestions in my head that I did not recognize. These were not malicious in any sense, however still disconcerting and shocking. Now I know that these were voices of the angelic realm and of the highest and best good, but at that time I was frightened by hearing voices other than my own inner dialogue. I was ready for that to be happening at the time, otherwise it wouldn't have happened, but fear jumped in and took control of my emotions, letting them run completely wild. While retrospectively looking at my own medical misdiagnosis, I received guidance that most people who are schizophrenic or who have other similar disorders are often experiencing things that are not of the third dimension, which we on Earth presently reside in. There are multiple dimensions or levels of reality that are typically not visible to humans, but exist simultaneously with our own. When people talk about Astral travelling, they are actually talking about playing in the 4th dimension, which is based in emotions. The fourth dimension is the space where unsettled beings reside, and for this reason, I do not advise astral travel. Together the third and fourth dimensions make up the "Lower Creation World". In this space, people feel separated from each other and from Spirit. This is also the arena in which any struggles around the concept of good versus evil are played out.

As this is the most spiritual chakra, food does not balance it as does the others. Food eaten with consideration to this chakra should be light, fresh food, filled with life-force energy. Eating the full spectrum of the rainbow supports the energy of this chakra. In doing this, you will be providing a strong base for the crown to stand upon. Liquids should be consumed regularly when working with this chakra it allows the energy to keep flowing throughout the body.

For the next three days, you will be focusing on your understanding of the world around you. Wearing purple or white clothing, purple or white jewelry and staying hydrated are great ways to flood it with extra energy as you are cleansing and clearing it. Meditation and conscious actions are the best ways to support the strength of this chakra.

<u>Day Nineteen:</u> Sahasrara, the crown chakra, connects you to Source and helps to cultivate understanding of our world. Think about 10 things that you understand and finish your thoughts below.

I understand _____

I understand _____

I understand _____

I understand _____

I understand _____

I understand _____

I understand _____

I understand _____

I understand _____

I understand _____

Did your list look like you thought it would when you started? Were there any surprises that came up when thinking about what you understand? Did you struggle to complete this list? Take some time to contemplate your responses and what they mean in regards to how you understand the world around you.

Day Twenty: How connected are you with Source? Take some time today to do some automatic writing, letting your pen do all the work, allowing your brain relax, asking the question, "what do I need to know from Source at this time?" Record your answer below.

_____

_____

_____

_____

_____

_____

_____

_____

_____

_____

_____

_____

_____

_____

_____

_____

_____

_____

_____

_____

_____

_____

<u>Day Twenty One:</u> Who am I? What do I believe about the universe? What do I believe about myself? Reflect on these questions and the past three days of focusing on your crown chakra.

_____

_____

_____

_____

_____

_____

_____

_____

_____

_____

_____

_____

_____

_____

_____

_____

_____

_____

_____

_____

_____

_____

_____

_____

_____

_____

_____

_____

_____

_____

_____

_____

_____

_____

_____

_____

_____

_____

_____

Take a look back at the questions listed in the beginning of the chapter. When you ask yourself the questions, are your answers still the same as they were the three days ago?

Congratulations!

YOU DID IT!

Congratulations! You did it! You took the time to learn about chakra and energy, but more importantly, you took the time to learn about and honor yourself. Take a moment to breathe that in. By spending just a few minutes each day checking into your chakra and your energy for the past 21 days, you have started a positive habit that will help you to lead a more connected existence.

Here's the other fun thing: you just meditated for 21 days! Each day's exercise consisted of a meditative practice along with some personal reflection, so those of you who doubted you could meditate, GREAT JOB! YOU DID IT!

ADDITIONAL TOOLS

CHAKRA MEDITATION

Find a comfortable position either seated or laying down, but do not allow yourself to become too relaxed, this meditation is designed to bring awareness to the body. Once you have found a comfortable position, allow yourself to feel the support beneath you. Connect with the ground below you and allow it support your body entirely. Take a deep breath in, and relax into your body. Exhale and allow your mind to soften. Notice the sounds around you, allowing them to float through your space without distraction. Bring your awareness to the light and the shade that surrounds you, feel the air dancing on the surface of your skin. Feel the sky above you, the Earth below supporting you. Give your mind permission to release what is not serving your highest and best good at this time. Take a deep breath in and on the exhale, release anything that is not yours. Draw your energy back into center, grounding yourself in this very moment. Slowly start to sense the space around you. With each rise and fall of your breath, become aware of its coming and going, the sensation as it passes between your lips, the sound it makes and natural warmth you exude.

Take a deep breath in, drawing the energy down to where your spine meets your tailbone at your root chakra. Breathe into your Root. Let it soften and gently expand on your breath, taking in nourishment and life force energy. Allow your root to connect deeply into the Earth, grounding yourself into her energy. Envision the color red bathing your root chakra, bringing it back into perfection.

When you are ready, allow your awareness to move up to your belly, just below your navel to your sacral chakra. Breathe into your Sacral, gently softening your body with each breath, taking in nourishment and life force energy. Envision the color orange enveloping your sacral chakra bringing it back into perfection.

When you are ready move your awareness up to the area between your navel and below your breast bone to your Solar Plexus - your chakra of personal power. Take a deep breath in allowing your solar plexus to soften and expand on your breath. Purify your Solar Plexus with the color of sunshine; replenishing, restoring and nurturing. Envision the yellow color of sunshine bathing your solar plexus, bringing it back to perfection.

In your own time, bring your awareness up to the center of your chest to your Heart chakra – the chakra of unconditional love. Gently breathe into your Heart space, letting it soften and expand with each breath. Immerse your heart with nourishment, renewal and healing. Envision your Heart chakra being bathed in first in green healing light and then enveloped in the soft pink light of unconditional love bringing the chakra back into perfection.

As you are guided, bring your awareness up to your throat chakra, the center of self expression and personal truth. Take a deep breath in, feeling your throat chakra open and expand with each breath. Let yourself release the need for control, and allow yourself to feel completely free using self-expression and creativity. Envision the color blue bathing your throat chakra, bringing it back into perfection.

When you are ready, bring your awareness up to your brow area to your Third Eye chakra, center of wisdom and intuition. Take a deep, cleansing breath in, feeling your chakra open and expanding, allowing yourself to find clarity, insight and understanding. Bathe your third eye chakra in the color indigo, soothing and balancing, bringing it back into perfection.

In your own time, as you are ready, move your awareness up to the top of your head to your Crown chakra, the connection to oneness. Take a deep breath in, feeling your chakra open and expand, allowing for harmony and restoration to take place. Envision a pure white light entering your crown, bathing you in Divine light bringing the chakra back into perfection.

When you are ready come back to yourself as a whole, start by acknowledging the ebb and flow of your breath. Breathe into your core. Remember you are perfect, whole and complete just as you are. In your own time, you can begin to come back to consciousness. Feel the air on your skin, notice the sounds around you. Start by wiggling your fingers and toes, slowly and consciously feeling your body. Thank yourself for taking this time to honor your body. And so it is.

FOOD

Food is one of the most important aspects of maintaining your personal energy. The old adage of "you are what you eat" is entirely accurate once you come to the understanding that everything is indeed energy. We eat to nourish our bodies, to provide the proper nutrition so that our bodies can continue producing miracles. One of the best things that you can do for yourself is to fuel your body properly, honoring your body as a sacred vessel by choosing healthy, fresh, and natural options.

It took me a long time to come to this understanding and heal my relationship with food. I was raised in an environment where my food intake was restricted. I was told what to eat, when to eat and how to eat it. I didn't put my own food on my plate or make decisions about what I chose to consume. As a result of this, when I went out, I would binge eat, which eventually led to purging. Once I started looking at the emotional aspect of my relationship with food, I was able to release the old beliefs that I was carrying inside me that connected food with guilt, shame and self-loathing. I was able to make the connection that the energy with which we consume the food has everything to do with how our body receives the nutrition of the food. I now understand that food is to be treated as fuel for the body, so that it can achieve its full potential. Food is not a reward or treat, but the vehicle which provides the body sustenance. Recently I have seen an image circulating on social media that perfectly summed up this idea stating, "Stop rewarding yourself with food. You are not a dog."

Cooking beautiful, healthy food has since become one of my passions. I love to challenge myself and see how many nutrient-rich items I can fit into one dish while maintaining a high caliber of execution. I try to buy whole, fresh foods (organic if possible and reasonable!) versus packaged and prepared. I do this for a number of reasons – the first being that I have had food allergies since childhood, so I have had to be consciousness of the ingredients in the food I consume. The second reason is that I like to control the flavor and the spice in my food. Not that I am picky, but there are certain things that I cannot stand in my food (I'm talking to you, cilantro, cumin and coriander). By preparing the majority of my own food, I can maintain that level of quality control that I desire. I also tend to find prepared food too salty for my tastes. Growing up, there was a point in time that I was taking Lithium pills in combination with other treatments for depression. Since taking the Lithium (which is a salt compound), I find my tastes being very sensitive to salt and sodium in food.

Cooking is all about creativity and adaptability. My cooking is entirely guided by intuition; I only use recipes when baking. I don't measure out amounts of ingredients or spices. I have been known to have full conversations with my Spirit guides while cooking, asking for advice on unknown food adventures. I am told that its quite entertaining to watch me cook, bake or fumble with my varied collection of kitchen appliances and utensils. I use what I have, what is readily available and what I am guided to include in a dish. I've made some interesting (and delicious!) food swaps for typical ingredients instead of purchasing a special ingredient. I typically cook a bunch of grains and veggies at once so that I have base ingredients to build from during the week. This way I don't have to work so hard when I am really hungry. I have found that when I don't have options available to throw something together quickly, that is when I turn to food that my stomach quickly regrets. Sometimes a snack for me is as simple as fresh mozzarella cheese with whatever roasted veggies I have in the fridge with a drizzle of balsamic reduction or just a handful of pretzels and dried cranberries. Even when I have food around that I don't love (who decides what flavors go in the 3-pack of yogurt anyways?), I find adding spices and extra love is a fast way to make your food palatable.

I should also mention that I am proponent of eating whatever you want, at the meal that you want. Now I am not saying to go ballistic and eat everything in your line of sight. What I mean is that you shouldn't categorize food only to be eaten at a specific time. If you wake up craving steak, have a steak for breakfast. Listen to your body and what it is telling you that it wants, when it wants. This is not license to go crazy and binge eat whatever you want; what I am asking you to do is check in with what your body wants before you make food choices, not your logical mind. Your body will tell you what it wants if you take the time to listen and honor it. There is no hard and fast rule that says you can only eat cereal between the hours of 5 and 9 am, so there should be nothing stopping you from eating the meal you want, when you want it. And let's be real, if your body does not appreciate what you've eaten it'll tell you!

When making changes in your diet, it is crucial to listen to your body and give it the proper support that it needs, in order to make the shifts that you are asking it to make. I have found out the hard way that for my body, gluten does not work. I had been tested many times for wheat allergies and various related conditions, but there was never any medical confirmation that told me to avoid gluten. Begrudgingly, one day, I listened to a dear friend when she recommended that I try to avoid gluten to see if it helped my stomach ailments. People kept telling me that I should try and eliminate it from my diet, but I was stubborn since I had previously tried to eliminate it for maybe a week at a time with no results. I had never actually stuck with anything long-term, but I was ready to try anything that would help me end my constant pain. Honestly, I didn't notice too much change at first, until I was about two weeks into my gluten-free adventure. I had lunch plans with a girlfriend from college, at one of our favorite hometown restaurants where I would normally go straight for a sandwich. One that would clearly be packed with delicious, delicious gluten. I had asked my guides for a sign that would indicate if I was supposed to indulge in what I wanted, or stick with my new dietary changes. That morning when I got out of the shower, I looked down at my arms and noticed that I was able to see the bones in my hands and the veins in my arms. I know this sounds trivial, but when your body is so consistently inflamed that these features are indistinguishable, it is quite noticeable when they do reappear. Of course, after seeing that I couldn't bring myself to eat a sandwich that day and I was *that person* who ordered a salad in a sandwich joint. Now when I do consume food with gluten, my body reacts almost instantaneously with a headache and upset stomach not far behind.

You may have noticed that there are a number of foods that work in tandem with the root chakra, but the amount of foods that work to balance the chakra decreases as you work your way up to the crown chakra. Building from a strong root, eating a full rainbow of colors will not only help to keep your chakra aligned, it will help you to maintain a healthy lifestyle. Each shade of the rainbow provides benefits of different vibrations, along with the full spectrum of vitamins and minerals that the body needs. The internet is a wonderful source of help when it comes to cooking and meal planning. I have found great success skimming websites like Pinterest for inspiration when I have unfamiliar ingredients. Over the few pages, I will share the foods that work in tandem with each chakra, along some of my favorite breakfasts, lunches, dinners and snack options and ideas that correlate to each. These are all food choices that I would make when I need an extra boost. You will find some space in each section to make note of your favorite foods too! I will be featuring some of the meal idea recipes on my website: www.ariellesterling.com .

ROOT CHAKRA SAMPLE FOODS

Root Vegetables:

arrowroot
beet
carrot
cassava / yucca
celeriac
daikon
dandelion
fennel
Jerusalem artichoke / sun choke
jicama
lotus root
onion
parsley
parsnip
potato
radish
rutabaga
shallot
taro
turnip
water chestnut
water lily
yam / sweet potato

Naturally Red Foods:

blood orange
cherry
cranberry
pomegranate
radicchio
red apple
red cabbage
red grapes
red pepper
red / pink grapefruit
rhubarb
strawberry
tomato
watermelon

Spices:

black pepper
cayenne pepper
cinnamon
garlic
ginger
ginseng
paprika
turmeric

ROOT CHAKRA SAMPLE MEALS

Breakfast
- Yogurt with pomegranate seeds
- Broiled pink grapefruit
- Hot cereal with strawberries, cranberries or cherries

Lunch
- Tomato or red pepper stuffed with tuna or egg salad
- Roasted beet salad
- Watermelon, feta and arugula salad

Dinner
- Chicken Paprikash (Hungarian pepper stew – an old family recipe)
- Baked potato or baked sweet potato with chili
- Quinoa-stuffed red peppers

Snack
- Red pepper sticks in hummus
- Strawberries in balsamic vinegar
- Chips and salsa

My favorite root chakra foods:

_____

_____

_____

_____

_____

_____

_____

_____

_____

_____

SACRAL CHAKRA SAMPLE FOODS

Fermented Food:

bread (sourdough)
cod liver oil
Crème fraîche
fish sauce
kefir
kimchi
kumbucha
miso
pickles
sauerkraut
some cheeses
sour cream
soy sauce
Tabasco sauce
tofu / tempeh
Worcestershire sauce
yogurt

Naturally Orange Foods:

apricot
butternut squash
cantaloupe
carrots
kumquat
mango
nectarine
orange
orange pepper
papaya
peach
persimmon
pumpkin
sweet potato
tangerine

Fats and Oils:
avocado oil
flaxseed oil
grape seed oil
olive oil

Nuts and Seeds:
almond
cashews
hazelnut
macadamia nut
peanut
pecan
walnut

pumpkin seeds
sesame seeds
sunflower seeds

Fish and Seafood:

anchovies
herring
mackerel
oysters
salmon
sardines
trout
tuna

Please note: These are not comprehensive lists, just some of the healthiest options in each category

SACRAL CHAKRA SAMPLE FOODS

Breakfast
- Fruit smoothies with orange and mango
- Sweet potato pancakes
- Pumpkin muffins

Lunch
- Butternut squash soup
- Miso soup with tofu and vegetables
- Cuban-style sweet potato salad

Dinner
- Grilled salmon and veggies
- Sesame shrimp and wok-seared veggies
- Sweet potato curry

Snack
- Carrot sticks in Greek yogurt onion dip
- Dried mango
- Pickles and olives

My favorite sacral chakra foods:

_____

_____

_____

_____

_____

_____

_____

_____

_____

SOLAR PLEXUS CHAKRA SAMPLE MEALS

Naturally Yellow Foods:

banana
corn
golden beet
lemon
peach
pineapple
spaghetti squash
summer squash
saffron
yellow onion
yellow pepper
yellow tomato

Whole Grains:

amaranth*
barley
buckwheat*
bulgur
corn*
farro
freekah
millet*
oats*
quinoa*
rice* / wild rice*
rye
sorghum*
spelt
teff*
wheat

*Gluten Free

Natural Sweeteners:

agave
blackstrap molasses
coconut sugar
date sugar
dates
maple syrup
raw honey

Warming Spices:

black pepper
cardamom
cayenne
cinnamon
garlic
ginger
horseradish
turmeric

Legumes:

alfalfa
black eyed pea
carob
chickpea (garbanzo bean)
clover
garden pea
kidney bean
lentil
lima bean
mung bean
peanuts
soybeans
tamarind

SOLAR PLEXUS CHAKRA SAMPLE MEALS

Breakfast
- Quinoa patty with egg on top
- Banana bread
- Fresh pineapple / pineapple juice

Lunch
- Pineapple fried rice
- Couscous salad with roasted veggies and a lemon vinaigrette
- Corn chowder

Dinner
- Spaghetti squash prepared as your favorite pasta
- Curried lentil stew
- Spanish Paella

Snack
- Hummus
- Blondies made with chickpeas
- Brownies made with black beans

My favorite solar plexus chakra foods:

_____

_____

_____

_____

_____

_____

_____

_____

_____

HEART CHAKRA SAMPLE FOODS

Naturally Green Vegetables:

artichoke
arugula
asparagus
bok choy
broccoli
brussel sprouts
cabbage / Napa cabbage
celery
collard greens
cucumber
garlic scape
green beans
green olives
green onions
green pepper
kale
lettuce
mustard greens
spinach
Swiss chard
tomatillo
zucchini

Green Herbs:

basil
cilantro
dill
oregano
parsley

Green Fruits:

avocado
green apple
green grapes
honeydew melon
kiwi
lime
pear
watermelon

Other Green Foods:

green tea
pistachios

HEART CHAKRA SAMPLE MEALS

Breakfast
- Fruit smoothie with kale or spinach
- Omelet with veggies
- Roasted asparagus and sunny side up eggs

Lunch
- Cucumber salad
- Asian inspired Zucchini noodle salad
- Spinach salad

Dinner
- Stuffed zucchini boats
- Veggie fajitas with tomatillo salsa
- Grilled fish with chimichurri sauce

Snack
- oven baked kale chips
- celery and nut butter
- avocado and sugar (this is a childhood favorite of mine, just needs a little bit of raw cane sugar to sweeten the fruit)

My favorite heart chakra foods:

_____

_____

_____

_____

_____

_____

_____

_____

_____

_____

THROAT CHAKRA SAMPLE FOODS

Naturally Blue Foods:
Blueberry
Blue corn
Blue potato

Liquids:
Water
Chamomile tea
Herbal tea
Peppermint tea
100% pure fruit juice

Foods that fall from a tree when ripe:
Apple
Peach
Pear
Apricot
Plum

THROAT CHAKRA SAMPLE MEALS

Breakfast
- hot cereal with blue berries
- yogurt with blueberries
- blue smoothies

Lunch
- vegetable soup
- salad with blueberry lemon vinaigrette
- Vietnamese Pho noodle soup

Dinner
- roasted chicken and tri colored potatoes
- salmon with a blueberry barbeque sauce
- blue corn nachos

Snack
- blueberry lemon bread
- blue corn chips and salsa
- dark chocolate peppermint bark

My favorite throat chakra foods:

_____

_____

_____

_____

_____

_____

_____

_____

_____

_____

THIRD EYE CHAKRA SAMPLE FOODS

Naturally Purple Foods: **Foods Rich in Omega-3s:**

black currants

blackberries

eggplant

elderberries

figs

plums

prunes

purple asparagus

purple cabbage

purple carrot

purple grapes

purple kohlrabi

purple pepper

purple potato

raisins

raspberries

chia seeds

cod liver oil

egg yolks

fish (mackerel, herring, salmon,
    tuna, whitefish, sardines, anchovies)

flax seeds

hemp seeds

salmon fish oil

walnuts

**Third Eye Foods to
Consume in Moderation:**

dark chocolate

red wine

THIRD EYE CHAKRA SAMPLE MEALS

Breakfast
- cinnamon raisin hot cereal
- yogurt with blackberries
- purple potato hash and eggs

Lunch
- purple cabbage and purple carrot slaw
- roasted purple vegetables
- deviled eggs

Dinner
- eggplant parmesan
- roasted salmon and purple asparagus
- Asian inspired spicy eggplant

Snack
- babaganoush (roasted eggplant dip)
- red grapes and cheese
- chia seed pudding

My favorite third eye chakra foods:

_____

_____

_____

_____

_____

_____

_____

_____

_____

CROWN CHAKRA SAMPLE FOODS

Breakfast
- rainbow smoothie
- roasted veggies and sunny side up eggs
- vegetable frittata

Lunch
- Buddha bowl
- Stir fry
- Veggie fajitas
- Rainbow wrap

Dinner
- Ratatouille
- Caprese salad
- Vegetable stew
- Rainbow sushi

Snack
- fruit salad
- miso soup
- rainbow veggie skewers

My favorite crown chakra foods:

_____

_____

_____

_____

_____

_____

_____

_____

_____

_____

WATER & HYDRATION

The human body is composed of at least 50% liquid water at any given time. Every individual is unique, with each bodies composition containing at times up to 75% water (babies and children), decreasing over time as the body transforms. Aside from water being nearly 20% of the blood's plasma, it has a number of vital responsibilities in the body. It is the primary building block of the body's cells (37.2 trillion of them in case you were wondering—I was). Lubricating the joints, water in the body acts as a shock absorber to your organs, in addition to insulating key organs such as the brain and spinal cord. There are many other compounds in the body that utilize water as a component, so there is often debate over how much water the body actually contains. Given this understanding of merely a few of the functions water has in your body, it is much easier to understand why it is so important to consume plenty of water and stay properly hydrated.

The body recognizes thirst after an individual has already lost about 2-3% of their hydration, however mental performance and physical coordination become impaired after a 1% hydration loss. If you are only drinking when you are thirsty, your body is already dehydrated. A lot of people that they don't drink water because they don't like the taste. I grew up in the Chicago area and there is nothing better than the taste of Lake Michigan tap water, but now living in here in Arizona, we don't drink the tap water, so I can appreciate when people say that water has a taste. Nonetheless, it is still important to hydrate properly. I prefer to drink water based drinks such as tea or lemonade versus anything artificially processed like soda, energy or sports drinks. I don't like the idea of added chemicals or dyes being added to anything I consume, so I do my best to stay away from those things.

A great way to add an extra punch of flavor to your water to help encourage regular consumption is to add fresh fruit, herbs or spices. I like constant variety so I tend to use a water bottle with a built in strainer, but feel free to brew a larger batch. This way it is ready for you to drink, and not just when you are thirsty! There is an endless amount of flavor combinations that can be made! Make sure to start with the best ingredients possible to achieve the best outcome: filtered water, the freshest fruit available, fresh herbs and whole spices are preferred. The more ingredients you use and the longer you let your water brew, the more flavorful your water will become. If you're easing into this idea a good place to start is with a neutral and comfortable flavor such as lemon or cucumber. By just letting a slice infuse into a glass of water, you are enjoying the subtle benefits of this chakra energy boost. I have also heard of people adding essential oils to their water, which I think is quite an interesting idea. The only thing I would say is to make sure that you are well versed, making sure that your oil is food grade and meant for human consumption. Below are some of the combinations that relate to each chakra either based on the fruit's color or the herb's energetic and medicinal properties.

ROOT
- Strawberry & basil
- Apple & cinnamon

SACRAL
- Orange & kiwi
- Mango & mint

SOLAR PLEXUS
- Lemon & rosemary
- Pineapple & mint

HEART
- Watermelon & mint
- Honeydew & basil

THROAT
- Blueberry & lime
- Lime & mint

THIRD EYE
- Blackberry & sage
- Raspberry & lime

CROWN
- Dragon fruit & cucumber
- Passion fruit & hibiscus

MY FAVORITE FLAVORED WATER COMBINATIONS:

_____

_____

_____

_____

_____

_____

_____

Another great option to hydrate that is popular in my home state of Arizona is called "agua fresca". This refreshing drink is lighter than a smoothie, but still more satisfying than tea or lemonade on a hot day. This beverage is created by blending any single fruit or a combination of fruits with water at approximately a 2:3 ratio, adding a small amount of a natural sweetener if needed. This drink can be strained or drank with a bit of texture. Popular varieties include watermelon and pineapple, but the possibilities are truly endless.

SALT BATHS

Salt baths are one of my favorite ways to clear and balance all my chakra simultaneously. These baths help to move energy and draw out any toxins and impurities in the system. I have heard that it is optimal to use at least 2 cups of pink Himalayan sea salt for this process, but I don't necessarily measure out as much as let my guidance tell me how much to add to the bath tub. I use the hottest water that I can stand, pink Himalayan sea salt, baking soda and whatever essential oil I am guided to use at the time. There are many different ways that you can draw a bath; do what your intuition guides you to do. If you do not have access to a bathtub, you can also use this solution as a soak for your feet. You can also use finely ground Himalayan sea salt mixed with your favorite lotion and rub it on your skin. As it exfoliates your skin, it also cleanses your energy field.

By using water that is hotter than your body's temperature, this allows for the toxins to be drawn to the surface of the skin. As the water gradually cools, the toxins are pulled into the water via the principle of osmosis. The hot water will also make you sweat profusely, moving liquid energy out through every pore of your body, from some places you didn't even know existed. Skin is the body's largest organ and has the most exposure to external elements making this one of the most important habits to get into. Using baking soda in addition to the salt helps to neutralize the chemicals in unfiltered water, primarily chlorine and also helps to increase mineral absorption through the skin. Pink Himalayan sea salt contains 84 essential minerals that nourish the body, but also mimic a mother's amniotic fluid, making the skin feel baby smooth.

STEPS TO CREATE A ENERGY CLEANSING BATH

1. Shower and thoroughly cleanse your body before taking your bath.
2. Fill the tub with water that is just at or above body temperature. The heat allows for maximum absorption of minerals and will make you sweat, allowing the body to release what no longer serves it.
3. Dissolve baking soda (approx. ½ cup) and pink Himalayan sea salt (approx. 2 cups) into the bath as the tub is filling. If you are using essential oils, you can add 10-15 drops at this time.
4. Soak in the tub for as long as is comfortable, at least 15 minutes, but not exceeding an hour.
5. Remember to stay hydrated while in the bath! You are losing profuse amounts of water when you sweat so it is important to replenish yourself.
6. When you are finished, drain the tub and get out <u>slowly</u>. You may feel tired and weak from all the energy that was released and that is perfectly okay!
7. Pat yourself dry. You do not want to shower and wash away all of the rich minerals that are soaking into your skin.
8. Thank yourself for taking the time to honor YOU.

Here are some of my favorite essential oil combinations for each chakra:

ROOT	Thieves Oil (Clove, Lemon, Cinnamon, Eucalyptus Radiata, and Rosemary)
SACRAL	Clary Sage and Sweet Orange
SOLAR PLEXUS	Lemon and Rosemary
HEART	Rose and Sandalwood
THROAT	Eucalyptus and Basil
THIRD EYE	Frankincense and Lavender
CROWN	Jasmine and Cedarwood

Salt baths can be taken up to three times per week to help keep energy moving and aid in releasing toxins. Regular baths may be taken at any time and can be turned into a relaxing spa bath with the addition of any essential oils.

HIMALAYAN SEA SALT

What is Himalayan sea salt and why is it so special? The most noticeably different aspect of this salt is its rich color, ranging anywhere from transparent to its most known pink, even to dark red. It is mined from the second largest salt mine in the world, Khewra Salt Mines in Pakistan, located at the foothills of the Himalayas. Perhaps the most unique aspect of this amazing salt is that it contains trace elements of 84 minerals. Regular salt is chemically NaCl or Sodium Chloride, only two elements: sodium and chlorine. In large chunks such as salt lamps, the mineral formation is known as Halite. This miraculous mineral can be utilized in many applications such as cooking, in health and beauty treatments and as a component in a salt lamp. Himalayan salt is considered to be healthier than regular salt since there are no additives, and it contains so many naturally occurring minerals that your body needs.

Salt lamps are a great way to cleanse and refresh the energy in any space that you spend time in! Salt lamps naturally cleanse the air around you, producing negative ions that help to balance out negative energies. Negative ions help to balance out positive ions that are put out by electronic devices (televisions, computers, etc.). Negative ions work to reduce germs in the air, so salt lamps are often recommended to people with asthma or other bronchial issues. An increase in negative ions increases the flow of oxygen to the brain creating a healthier environment for the body.

The list below contains the full list of the 82 minerals that are found in the Himalayan salt in addition to the standard sodium and chloride.

Actinium	Hafnium	praseodymium
Aluminum	Holmium	protactinium
Antimony	Hydrogen	radium
Arsenic	Indium	rhenium

astatine
barium
Beryllium
Bismuth
Boron
bromine
cadmium
calcium
carbon
cerium
cesium
chromium
cobalt
copper
dysprosium
erbium
europium
fluorine
francium
gadolinium
gallium
germanium
Gold

Iodine
Iridium
Iron
lanthanum
lead
lithium
lutetium
magnesium
manganese
mercury
molybdenum
neodymium
neptunium
nickel
niobium
nitrogen
osmium
oxygen
palladium
phosphorus
platinum
plutonium
polonium
potassium

rhodium
rubidium
ruthenium
samarium
scandium
selenium
silicon
silver
Strontium
Sulfur
Tantalum
Tellurium
Terbium
Thallium
Thorium
Thulium
Tin
Titanium
Uranium
Vanadium
Wolfram
Yttrium
Ytterbium
Zinc
Zirconium

Please note that even though you may see elements that are not meant for human consumption, there are only trace amounts and no where near a toxic levels.

COLOR THERAPY

Have you ever wondered what color really is? Color is determined by frequency; it is the visible expression of light at varying wave lengths (frequencies). Frequency is the rate at which a vibration (sound, light, radio, etc.) creates a wave. Each color of the visible spectrum, commonly referred to as ROYGBIV, corresponds to a point in the chakra system, starting at the root and moving up to the crown. By building on this knowledge, we start to understand that everything is energetically intertwined and we can alter our own energy using different vibrations.

Think about all of the ways that color is used as an expression and how color surrounds your life already. For example, red stop signs are designed to bring attention to ground ourselves in the moment and pay attention to what's going on around us. Once you start to pay closer attention to how color is used, you may start to notice more synchronicities. For instance, how doctors offices are often painted light, soothing shades of green to help facilitate healing energy.

There are a number of ways that you can incorporate the healing energy of colors into your daily experience. Maybe you'll find a red mat to sit on while meditating. Or perhaps, you'll paint a wall blue in your office to help you focus on clear communication. Wearing specific colors in clothing, shoes and jewelry is a great way to utilize color therapy on a daily basis to boost your chakra, but the possibilities are truly endless. There are a number of technological advances can assist you in providing color therapy in new and unique ways in the comfort of your own home. There are a variety of light bulbs that can change to any color of the spectrum, making these great not only for mood lighting, but to be able to bathe the entire room (and it's energetic contents: people, pets, crystals, plants, etc.) in a specific color. My favorite new application are the shower heads that have a built in lights that cycles through all of the colors of the rainbow. This application acts as a chakra double whammy by bathing your entire being in light and cleansing it in water simultaneously. Another great time-tested option is a light box. This is a portable device that replicates the sun's balanced light spectrum. This tool is often prescribed to individuals who suffer from Seasonal Affective Disorder (SAD) and who may benefit from extra sunlight.

Color and light have a much larger impact on our lives than we consider. Recently, tech giant Apple has added a setting to dim the blue lights on their mobile devices between the hours of 10 pm and 7 am to help promote more restful sleep. Other tech companies have started to follow suit, looking deeper into the affects of the blue light on our brain function. Personally, I find myself very sensitive to ANY light, both natural and artificial. I do not have any traditional lighting in my bedroom; it is too obtrusive on my senses, especially as a clairvoyant. I use a combination of overhead black lights, lava lamps and salt lamps. Not only does this make me feel like I live in a genie lamp, but this combination provides me with enough light to see without overwhelming my sensitive eyes. This also allows my eyes to remain at what I would consider to be an optimal level of light allowance for clairvoyance. I find that I am able to see energy much more clearly at this darker level. I do notice that the nights that I accidentally fall asleep with the black lights on, my dreams seem to be more vivid as it charges the third eye chakra.

In the back of this book, you will notice that there are some mandalas and other geometric shapes to color. Coloring is a recently popularized form of mediation and is a great way to relax and unwind. Adult coloring books are now readily available wherever books are sold. I have also included a chart that indicates possible connections to the colors that you may be drawing with (related to your chakra of course!).

EXERCISE

Exercise was my biggest foe, my arch nemesis. When something like exercise and fitness is forced upon you, there can be a certain level of distain that clouds any benefits that you may be receiving from it. Every time I exercised I would be full of anger and resentment, which created layers of anger and resentment trapped in my body. Just like anything else, the energy in which we perform an action is the energy you receive in return, not necessarily the actual prescribed benefits. It took years for me to make this connection, and come to the understanding that exercise had nothing to do with losing weight, as many of us have been brought up to believe. Let me repeat that, exercise has nothing to do with losing weight.

Once I had shifted my perspective on exercise, I came to the understanding that exercise was intended to move energy throughout the body. The excess weight that had been hanging around my middle started to fall off once I made this connection and starting doing the emotional work, not just focusing on the diet and exercise aspects of being healthy. I am not the kind of person who enjoys the gym experience like some people do. Staring at myself in a mirror while I work up a sweat, is not my idea of a fun time, so I tend to gravitate towards outdoor activities. I typically don't exercise with other people, but meeting up with friends to go hiking or walk around a street fair or farmers market never feels forced. The most important thing about exercise is that you find something that you enjoy doing and just do it!

The universe provides us opportunities to do what our bodies need as long as we pay attention to the signs. For example, there are days when I'll ask for exercise to be built into my day and then, mysteriously, there aren't any parking spaces and I'm taking a nice scenic walk. Or those times when we don't want to do squats, but end up having to pull weeds instead, those situations are more than just coincidence. Don't discount those little synchronicities and the universe chiming in as to what energies need to be moved around in the body!

Yoga, qigong and tai chi are all Eastern meditative practices specifically designed with the intention of moving energy through the body. Therefore, these are all fantastic opportunities to work with the chakra system. Local community and recreation centers and community colleges are great places to look for classes if you aren't familiar with any studios in your area that offer these modalities. The internet is a fantastic resource for finding classes near you. There are also many practitioners who offer online classes through various online streaming channels.

SOUND HEALING

Sound healing can come in many forms. Think about how many times in your life you surrounded yourself with music and let yourself experience the emotions that otherwise could not be felt. As a teenager, I locked myself in my room often, letting music wash over me, taking away the intense emotions that I felt for the world around me. I relied heavily on sound healing, even though I had no idea that that actually was. Sound healing is the idea that sound and vibration are powerful, healing instruments that can be used as a tool to change energy when observed audibly.

Understanding the terminology in regards to sound can help to better explain its practical application for healing. Sound occurs when the frequency range is at an audible level. Frequency is the rate of speed at which the mechanism vibrates (a string on a guitar, the covering of a drum, etc.). The term frequency is synonymous with the term pitch in regards to sound and music. The unit used is Hertz, abbreviated as Hz, and refers to the amount of vibrations are occurring each second.

Sound healing has been used as a tool for centuries in a wide variety of applications. Traditional mantras were created with respect to the vibrational resonance of sacred words and phrases. By rhythmically chanting or repeating mantras, they are absorbed and resonate throughout each cell of the body affecting change at a core level. In speaking a mantra, you are taking an active role in sound healing. Affirmations are the modern answer to traditional mantras acting as encouraging statements used for intrinsic motivation.

Crystal healing bowls are specially crafted out of quartz crystal to resonate at specific frequencies. The sound comes from the striker or mallet when struck or rubbed against the bowl, creating sounds based on the size and shape of the bowl. Bowls are created to resonate with the Universal Harmony frequencies of each chakra. This is one of my favorite alternative healing modalities as I can feel the sound waves within my body.

Crystal bowls are fairly expensive and specialized tools, so this is not a common household item. Many yoga and mediation studios feature crystal bowl healing sessions. There are also a number of crystal singing bowl meditations that can be found on the internet in case you can't find a local option. Himalayan or Tibetan singing bowls are similar to the crystal singing bowls, the main difference being the size and material used for the bowls. Tibetan bowls are typically smaller sized pieces, often handmade of bronze.

The Solfeggio frequencies are an ancient musical scale of six ascending notes that has been used in sacred music since medieval times. Each of the six frequencies serves a difference role in balancing the mind, body and spirit. One of the most well-known applications of the Solfeggio frequencies are the Gregorian chants. See the chart below for details on each of these frequencies and the affect that it can have on your healing. Often times, I will use this information when determining what music to use during a healing session. The intention of the frequency allows for a deeper healing experience.

UT	396 Hz	Liberating guilt and fear
RA	417 Hz	Undoing situations and facilitating change
MI	528 Hz	Transformation and miracles (DNA repair)
FA	639 Hz	Connecting/Relationships
SOL	741 Hz	Awakening Intuition
LA	852 Hz	Returning to Spiritual Order

This comprehensive chart of identifies the frequency and color of each musical note. This information fascinated me as this would allow for the translation of music into artwork and vice versa.

NOTE	HERTZ	COLOR
A	440	Orange-yellow
A♯	457.75	Yellow-orange
B♭	472.27	Yellow
B	491.32	Yellow-green
C♭	506.91	Green-yellow
B♯	511.13	Green
C	527.35	Green
C♯	548.62	Green-blue
D♭	566.03	Blue-green
D	588.86	Blue
D♯	612.61	Blue-violet
E♭	632.05	Violet-blue
E	657.54	Violet
F♭	678.41	Ultra Violet
E♯	684.06	Invisible Violet
F	705.77	Invisible Red
F♯	734.23	Infra Red
G♭	757.53	Red
G	788.08	Red-orange
G♯	819.87	Orange-red
A♭	845.89	Orange

♯ = sharp

♭ = flat

MEDITIATION & MINDFULNESS

One of the best explanations that I have heard about the word meditation is that it should be likened to the word sports. The term sports broadly encompasses a variety of activities (baseball, soccer, golf, etc.), as does the concept of meditation; there are a number of methods that are all considered meditation.

Here are some traditional types of meditation (this is certainly not a comprehensive list, just enough to get some ideas flowing for you):

ॐ **Zen** is a Japanese meditation that is done while seated in the lotus (sitting with crossed legs) position, while focusing on breathing. This tradition is rooted in Chinese Buddhism.

ॐ **Vipassana** meditation focuses on mindfulness and breathing while acknowledging bodily sensations and mental phenomena. This is done by observing moment to moment, but not clinging to any one thought. Vipassana is Pali for "insight" or "clear seeing". Pali is the sacred language of Theravada Buddhism.

ॐ A **metta** meditation encourages loving and kindness towards yourself, then others, then the entire universe. Metta means "kindness, benevolence, goodwill" in Pali.

ॐ A **mantra** meditation uses a word or phrase as a tool for focus. The vibration of the word or phrase is what is important for this tradition. One of the most commonly known mantra is *om shanti om* means something to the extent of: peace to all mankind, peace for all living and non living things, peace for the universe and peace for everything in cosmic manifestation. The mantra is typically repeated either 108 or 1008 times, counting while using *mala* beads to keep track.

ॐ The goal of **yoga** is spiritual purification and self-awareness. The *asanas* are poses, and *pranayama* are breathing exercises that encourage your body, mind and spirit to come into alignment. There are a number of meditative aspects you may already be familiar with:

- O **Chakra** meditations focus on balancing the seven main energy portals in your energy body.
- O A **third eye** meditation concentrates on the *anja* or brow chakra to tap into clairvoyant or other psychic abilities.
- O **Kundalini** meditation highlights the complex system of the awakening of Kundalini energy. *(Please note: this should only be practiced with a qualified yogi)*

ॐ **Qigong** is an ancient Chinese mind and body exercise for health and meditation that marries martial arts training with over 80 different types of breathing exercises.

ॐ A **religious** meditation is often encountered in Judeo-Christian cultures and can take the form of:

- O A contemplative prayer to God or a religious figure such as a Saint, an Angel or another Ascended Master.
- O Contemplative reading of spiritual or religious texts.
- O Sitting with God or another religious figure.

ॐ A **guided meditation** allows for outside assistance in reaching a meditative state. This can be done in a group or in an individual setting. Any type of meditation can be guided by another individual, but some of the most popular types are:

- O **Guided imagery** is when the leader takes you on a journey to a different place (beach, meadow, forest, etc.) Or even a different point in time (ancient Egypt or the future, for example).
- O **Relaxation & body scans** aim to address and release any discomfort in the body while promoting healing and relaxation.
- O One of the most interesting applications of guided meditation coupled with modern technology is the use of **binaural beats.** This is a technique that presents two different frequencies to the brain, which then forces the brain to reconcile the difference. This process generates alpha waves (10 hz) which is associated with initial levels of meditation. This is often done by listening to a track while wearing headphones.

105

So now that I just gave you all those different types of meditation, I am going to share a little secret. I don't think that it really matters what type of meditation you do. The word meditation is often coupled with the term mindfulness. Personally, I feel that the act of meditation is however you choose to interpret the practice of mindfulness. Mindfulness is being present and in the moment, allowing yourself to observe your thoughts and feelings from a distance without judging them, good or bad. This happens when you allow yourself to experience flow, or complete absorption with an activity. Mihaly Csikszentmihalyi, Hungarian psychologist, describes flow as "being completely involved in an activity for its own sake. The ego falls away. Time flies. Every action, movement, and thought follows inevitably from the previous one, like playing jazz. Your whole being is involved, and you're using your skills to the utmost." (if you haven't heard of him, check out his Ted Talk on flow!) Most people experience flow in their daily lives without realizing it, whether it is during exercise (running, hiking, biking, etc.) or artistic endeavors (writing, art, cooking, etc.), we are already achieving this illusive meditation experience without knowing!

What I do think is important when actively meditating is setting an intention for your time. Your intent can be as simple as relaxing, or letting go of daily stress and clearing your mind, to more specific focuses (a spiritual journey or raising your personal vibration). Obviously your intent will control your experience and every meditation is unique, but when you set your intention for purposeful meditation you may hear, see or even feel things that are outside of your regular perceptions. Even if you don't experience any of these things during your meditation, know that you got exactly what you needed out of the time you took to honor yourself.

Here are a few proven effects that meditation has on your body:
- ॐ Better brain and immune function
- ॐ Lower blood pressure
- ॐ Lower blood cortisol levels
- ॐ Improved blood circulation
- ॐ Lower heart rate
- ॐ Less perspiration
- ॐ Slower respiratory rate
- ॐ Less anxiety
- ॐ Less stress

ॐ Deeper relaxation

ॐ Improved feelings of well-being

MANTRAS & AFFIRMATIONS

A mantra is a word or a sound that is spoken in repetition as a meditative aid. This is a sacred sound that is believed to have psychological and spiritual powers. Ancient Hindu mantras were symphonic and mathematically calculated based on sound and vibration. Affirmations are commonly used today much for the same purpose with the words carrying special significance.

There are a number of ways that affirmations can be incorporated into daily life:

ॐ Computer/phone/tablet backgrounds and lock screens

ॐ Sticky notes on desk or computer monitor or car dash

ॐ Writing in a dry erase marker (or lipstick!) on a mirror

ॐ Setting phone alarms with mantras

ॐ Meditation on a mantra/affirmation

ॐ Journaling feelings that are brought up with a mantra

ॐ Automatic writing starting with a mantra

ॐ Used while exercising to obtain deep focus

Over the next few pages you will find affirmation statements that are connected with each chakra. Some may resonate with you, some may not. Feel free to use the ones that you resonate with and are guided to. Once you are comfortable with the idea of affirmations, I encourage you to create your own mantras that resonate precisely to your unique vibration. There is no right or wrong way to use an affirmation, as long as you resonate with its message, it is yours.

Root Chakra Affirmations:

I am a divine being of light. I am peaceful, protected and secure.

I am connected to my body.

I am deeply rooted.

I am grateful for all the challenges that have helped me to grow and transform.

I am grounded and stable.

I am open to possibilities.

I am perfect, whole and complete just as I am.

I am safe and secure.

I am.

I have exactly what I need.

I love life.

I make choices that are healthy and good for me.

I nurture my body with healthy food, clean water, exercise, relaxation, and connection with nature.

I stand for my values, for truth, and for justice.

I trust in the goodness of life.

I trust myself.

Just like a tree or a star, I have a right to be here.

My Affirmations:

_____

_____

_____

_____

_____

_____

_____

Sacral Chakra Affirmations:

Emotions are the language of my soul.

I allow myself to experience pleasure.

I am open to experiencing the present moment through my senses.

I am open to touch and closeness.

I am passionate.

I am radiant, beautiful and strong and enjoy a healthy and passionate life.

I feel pleasure and abundance with every breath I take.

I feel.

I have healthy boundaries.

I know how to take care of my needs.

I love and enjoy my body.

I nourish my body with healthy food and clean water.

I take good care of my physical body.

I value and respect my body.

My sexuality is sacred.

My Affirmations:

_____

_____

_____

_____

_____

_____

_____

Solar Plexus Chakra Affirmations:

I act.

I am at peace with myself.

I am authentic.

I am free to choose in any situation.

I am positively empowered and successful in all my ventures.

I am proud of my achievements.

I am strong and courageous.

I am worthy of love, kindness, and respect.

I appreciate my strengths.

I choose healthy relationships.

I choose the best for myself.

I direct my own life.

I express myself in a powerful way.

I feel my own power.

I honor myself.

I love and accept myself.

I seek opportunities for personal and spiritual growth.

I stand up for myself.

My Affirmations:

_____

_____

_____

_____

_____

_____

_____

_____

Heart Chakra Affirmations:

All love resides within my heart.

I accept things as they are.

I am connected with other human beings.

I am grateful for all the challenges that helped me to transform and open up to love.

I am open to love and kindness.

I am open to love.

I am love.

I am peaceful.

I am wanted and loved.

I deeply and completely love and accept myself.

I feel a sense of unity with nature and animals.

I forgive myself.

I live in balance, in a state of gracefulness and gratitude.

I love the beauty of nature and the animal world.

I love.

I nurture my inner child.

Love is the answer to everything in life, and I give and receive love effortlessly and unconditionally.

My Affirmations:

_____

_____

_____

_____

_____

_____

_____

Throat Chakra Mantras:

I am at peace.

I am open, clear, and honest in my communication.

I communicate my feelings with ease.

I express my gratitude towards life.

I express myself creatively through speech, writing, or art.

I have a right to speak my truth.

I have a strong will that lets me resolve my challenges.

I speak with integrity.

I know when it is time to listen.

I listen to my body and my feelings to know what my truth is.

I live an authentic life.

I love to share my experiences and wisdom.

I nourish my spirit through creativity.

I speak my highest trurh.

I speak.

I take good care of my physical body.

My thoughts are positive, and I always express myself truthfully and clearly.

My Affirmations:

_____

_____

_____

_____

_____

_____

_____

Third Eye Chakra Mantras:

I am connected with the wisdom of the universe.

I am in touch with my inner guidance.

I am open to inspiration and bliss.

I am the source of my truth and my love.

I am tuned into the divine universal wisdom and always understand the true meaning of life situations.

I am wise, intuitive, and connected with my inner guide.

I forgive myself.

I forgive the past and learn what was there for me to learn.

I know that all is well in my world.

I listen to my deepest wisdom.

I listen to the wisdom of elders.

I love and accept myself.

I nurture my spirit.

I see.

I seek to understand and to learn from my life experiences.

I trust my intuition.

My life moves effortlessly.

My Affirmations:

_____

_____

_____

_____

_____

_____

_____

_____

Crown Chakra Mantras:

I am complete and one with the divine energy.

I am connected with the wisdom of the universe.

I am grateful for all the goodness in my life.

I am open to divine wisdom.

I am open to letting go of my attachments.

I am part of the Divine.

I cherish my spirit.

I honor the Divine within me.

I know that all is well in my world.

I listen to the wisdom of universe.

I live in the present moment.

I love and accept myself.

I seek experiences that nourish my spirit.

I seek to understand and to learn from my life experiences.

I trust my intuition.

I understand.

My life moves with grace and ease.

My Affirmations:

_____

_____

_____

_____

_____

_____

_____

_____

A NOTE ON FINDING A PRACTITIONER

I am a firm believer that everyone can heal themselves. The body is a miraculous being that has innate powers to work miracles, as long as you provide it the proper opportunities to heal. That being said, ask for help when you need help! Practitioners come in many forms so it is important to understand what you are looking for when you are looking for someone. Yoga practitioners, licensed massage therapists (LMT), Reiki practitioners, and many other types of light workers can help to balance out the chakra system and provide other support to the energy body.

You will be guided to the right practitioner. Friends and family are a great source for recommendations of people that are already known – try asking for a recommendation on your social media pages and see what comes up! There is no governing board of chakra healing if you will, so there isn't an organization to gather everyone who provides these types of services. The internet can be a great source to find practitioners as well, again, using your own discernment and intuition about whether or not your feel comfortable with an energy.

In my experience, the best practitioners are those who help you help yourself. What I mean by this is that they want to give you the tools for you to grow and learn for yourself, not just give you a quick fix for your issues. I am always cautious if someone tells me that they go to the same person on a regular basis for the same issues. As a practitioner, I want to empower my clients to grow and improve their lives, not keep them coming to me for the same problem.

There has to be a level of trust between you and your practitioner. This is something that can only be discerned by you and only you. Trust your instincts on this one. If a practitioner says something that you do not resonate with, then trust your own intuition. If see a practitioner doing something that you do not resonate with, trust your intuition. If a practitioner says one thing and does another, then they are likely out of alignment with themselves. No matter what, you should always feel comfortable with the people that you surround yourself with, especially the ones that you seek help from.

The proximity to your practitioner should not be a concern. Some people prefer to see someone locally for the experience, but this is entirely optional! Technology has certainly aided in easier facilitation of this concept, with options such as video conferencing helping to allow people to connect more personally. Since the chakras are apart of the bodies' subtle energy system, a practitioner who is an energy worker will be able to connect with your energy from a distance.

CHAKRA PENDULUM CHART

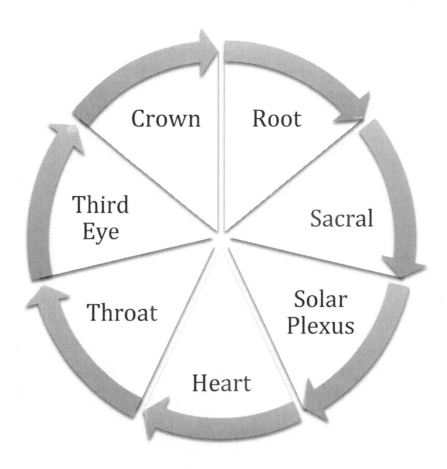

This is a tool that can be used with a pendulum to help discern if there is a question as to which chakra is causing a specific concern.

Please see www.ariellesterling.com for more information on using a pendulum.

EXTRA JOURNAL PAGES

COLORING PAGES

You will find a number of mandalas and other geometric shapes to color. There is no right or wrong, just artistic expression. Use the chart below to look deeper into what your art may be telling you.

Chakra	Color	Qualities
Root	Red	Love, energy, power, strength, passion, heat
Sacral	Orange	Courage, confidence, friendliness, success
Solar Plexus	Yellow	Bright, energy, sun, creativity, intellect, happy
Heart	Green	Money, growth, fertility, freshness, healing
Throat	Blue	Tranquility, loyalty, security, trust, intelligence
Third Eye	Indigo	Intuition, perception, devotion, wisdom, justice, fairness
Crown	Purple	Royalty, nobility, spirituality, luxury, ambition
	White	Goodness, innocence, purity, fresh, easy, clean

ACKNOWLEDGMENTS

Thank you to all my teachers.
Everyone who has crossed my path has brought with them a lesson.
Cheers to the teachers who have taught me love and compassion,
the teachers who taught me the lessons neither one of us wanted to learn,
and the teachers who showed me how to discover me.
Thank you to *all* of my teachers.

ABOUT THE AUTHOR

Arielle Sterling is an intuitive energy healer, certified Mind Body Spirit Practitioner, empath and Reiki Master. From a young age, Arielle knew she was different, having been keenly aware of her clairvoyant and clairaudient abilities and using them to help facilitate healing over a decade before she acquired any formal training. Her psychic abilities became overwhelming and intense, eventually asking for her gifts to go away until the point in time that she could understand and utilize them with grace and ease.

Arielle received her first Reiki attunement in 2004 and has immersed herself in mastering holistic therapies since. She has studied a multitude of energy therapies including: Usui Reiki, Therapeutic Touch® , Matrix Healing Technique: Electromagnetic Field & Body Integration, Lightbody Connection & Activation, DNA Cell(f) Imagery & Communication, and Spiritual Surgery. Arielle has studied with world-renowned psychic mediums, intuitive healers, angel communicators and astrologists to advance her own psychic and mediumship gifts. Her wide variety of modalities provides for a unique healing experience for every client.

Arielle's connection with the Ascended Masters, the Archangels, faeries and other her other guides allows her to be a conduit of positive energy, bringing love and healing to those who are ready and willing to receive it. She is often told that her sparkly and magnetic personality brings a soothing sense of peace and calm to those around her. Arielle would be honored to be apart of your journey to find what makes you lighter, brighter and happier because you deserve it.

For additional information or to request a personal session with Arielle, please visit www.ariellesterling.com

Made in the USA
San Bernardino, CA
08 July 2016